Logic Puzzles

Michellejoy Hughes

OXFORD
UNIVERSITY PRESS

OXFORD
UNIVERSITY PRESS

Great Clarendon Street, Oxford, OX2 6DP, United Kingdom

Oxford University Press is a department of the University of Oxford.
It furthers the University's objective of excellence in research, scholarship,
and education by publishing worldwide. Oxford is a registered trade mark
of Oxford University Press in the UK and in certain other countries

Text © Oxford University Press 2018

Author: Michellejoy Hughes

British Library Cataloguing in Publication Data
Data available

978-0-19-276953-4

10 9 8 7 6 5 4 3 2 1

Paper used in the production of this book is a natural, recyclable product
made from wood grown in sustainable forests. The manufacturing process
conforms to the environmental regulations of the country of origin.

Printed in China

Acknowledgements

Cover illustrations by Holly Fulbrook
Page make-up and illustrations by James Hunter

Although we have made every effort to trace and contact all copyright
holders before publication this has not been possible in all cases. If notified,
the publisher will rectify any errors or omissions at the earliest opportunity.

Hi Puzzle Fan,

Are you ready to test your brain power? This book is packed full of picture, word and number puzzles. Sharpen your pencil and let's kick-start your brain with these logic-puzzle challenges.

There are puzzles here for everyone so if you like…

- secret codes and picture challenges
- number puzzles and word searches
- jokes and riddles and clever tricks
- drawing and crafty ideas
- spot-the-difference and matching pairs

…there will be lots of things here you will **love**.

Along the way you will meet some interesting characters, ponder over riddles and crack plenty of codes.

How to use this book

In this book there are three sections of puzzles – warm-up, intermediate and tricky. They get more challenging as you progress through the book. Follow the simple introduction at the start of each puzzle and use a pencil in case you need to rub anything out. Try the quick quiz at the end of each section to see how much you remember and add up your score to discover your puzzle power.

By the end of the book you will have fine-tuned your logical thinking and boosted your problem-solving skills. That means increased brain power too!

You can find the answers at the back of the book, but don't look until you have completed the puzzles! A notepad is included on some pages in case you need space to help you work out the answer.

 We've put in some puzzle pointers to give you a clue so look out for the jigsaw symbol.

So what are you waiting for? Let's get going on some puzzle challenges...

Warm-up puzzles

1 Monster mash-up

The monster-making machine has gone mad. All of the monsters are mixed up and they each have parts of each other. What a mess!

Work out which parts are needed for each monster then draw them as they should be.

Monster 1: I'm all around like a roundabout. Put me back together again to help me keep my smile.

Monster 2: I'm a bit of a square sometimes. Help to get me back in shape and feeling good again.

Monster 3: I'm your pentagon-loving, five-a-day monster. Put me back together again and I will be very happy.

2 What did I wear?

I've made a code of what I wore last week. Solve the code then draw what I wore on Friday.

Monday: ALX

 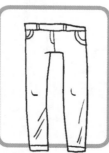 

Tuesday: BMX

 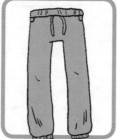 

Wednesday: BNY

 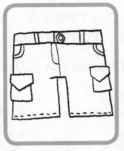 

Thursday: CLZ

Friday: AMY

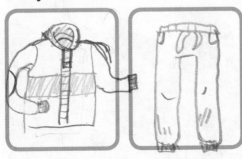 

When they walk around the zoo, visitors usually see the animals in the same order.

Circle the line that shows the different order.

1.

2.

3.

4.

5.

4 Pairs 1

Draw lines to connect each pair of identical shapes, making sure that no line touches another. You can only draw lines that are horizontal or vertical, not diagonal. The first one has been done for you.

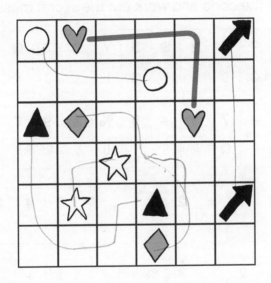

What fruit do twins like to eat?

Pears!

11

People have used secret codes for thousands of years. It is called **cryptology** which means 'secret writing'. This means messages can be sent to other people without anyone else knowing what has been written.

Look at the code and work out the secret message.

!	1	?	#	2	$	3	/	*	4	@	5	\
A	B	C	D	E	F	G	H	I	J	K	L	M

"	6	–	7	=	+	8	%	&	9	£	^	10
N	O	P	Q	R	S	T	U	V	W	X	Y	Z

+	2	?	=	2	8
s	e	c	r	e	t

?	6	#	2	+
c	o	d	e	s

!	=	2
a	r	e

$	%	"
f	u	n

!	+
a	s

^	6	%
y	o	u

?	!	"
c	a	n

\	!	@	2
m	a	k	e

!	"	^
a	n	y

\	2	+	+	!	3	2
m	e	s	s	a	g	e

2	"	?	=	^	–	8	2	#
e	n	c	r	y	p	t	e	d

6 Mixed messages 1

There is a message here. Work out what it says by rearranging the spaces between the words.

Ca nyo ure adt hi sme s sa ge
e ve nwh eni tlo okss ost ran ge?

Can you read this message even
when it looks so strange?

7 Cool running

Grab a notebook and in the bottom right corner of the page, draw a square and in it a stick person about to do something like walk, run, ride a bike, jump off a diving board, eat a meal – anything you like. On the next pages, in exactly the same corner space, add the next step of the action and keep doing this for as many pages as you want. Each time, think about how the stick person would move in little changes of action. Once you are done, flick through the pages of the notebook and watch your stick person move.

13

8 Owl's vowels 1

The owl has pinched the vowels from these bird names. Rewrite them with the vowels in the correct place to make the names of 12 well-known birds.

1. r b n   _robin_
2. s p r r w   _sparrow_
3. b l c k b r d   _blackbird_
4. b l t t   _blue tit_
5. g l d f n c h   _goldfinch_
6. s t r l n g   _starling_
7. p g n   _pigon_
8. d v   _dove_
9. c h f f n c h   _chaffinch_
10. w r n   _wren_
11. m g p   _magpie_
12. c r w   _crow_

Puzzle Pointer

If you aren't sure, look for common word endings (e.g. ing) or groups of letters (e.g. ch).

VOWELS

9 Star burst 1

Draw lines around the stars in the box so they are in groups of four. Each star can only be in one group and there must be 1 black star in every group.

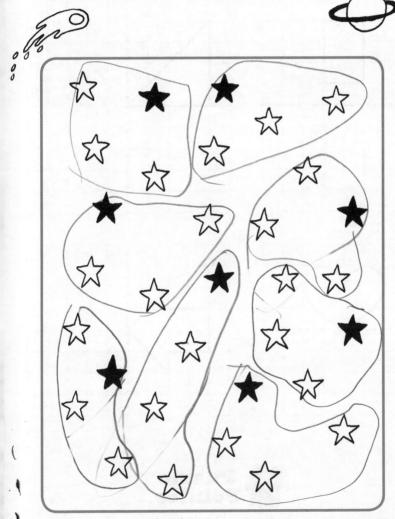

10 Mirror, mirror on the wall

Here are some shapes with a dotted mirror line. Draw the reflection that you would expect to see.

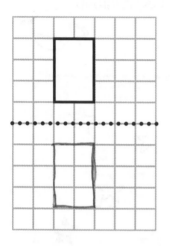 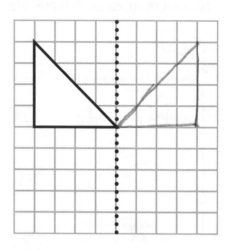

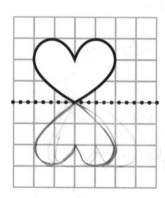 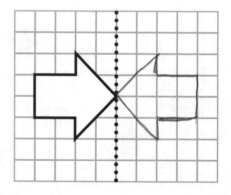

 **Puzzle Pointer**

Use the grid to help you by counting the squares.

11 Shape-shifter 1

How many triangles can you find in the shape below?
Write the number in the answer box.

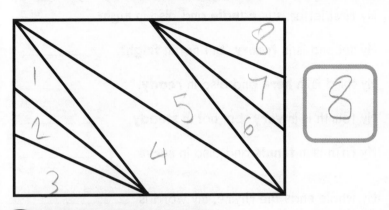

12 Box clever

Look around where you are now and try drawing
what you see in shapes. Don't put in any details or
texture, just shapes. For example, a person's body
might be several rectangles and an oval for a head.

Start with the big
shapes and then
add more shapes
for smaller parts.

Show your picture
to a friend. Can they
work out what it is?

17

13 Riddle and rhyme 1

Solve the clues to find the missing word.

My first letter is in **candle** and also in **night**. ___n___

My second is in **frenzy**, but not in **fright**. ___e___

My third is in **here** and also in **ready**. ___er___

My fourth is in **very**, but not in **steady**. ___vr___

My fifth is in **tennis** and also in **serve**. ___es___

My whole ends the rhyme, my word is ___nerve___

Puzzle Pointer

There will be more than one letter option for each clue
so write them all down and then work out what word
can be made. The letters will stay in the same order
as the clues. The answer rhymes with **serve**.

? Try this riddle: ?

What goes up when
rain comes down?

18

14 Follow the clues 1

ABCDEFGHIJKLMNOPQRSTUVWXYZ
BCDEFGHIJKLMNOPQRSTUVWXZA

If the code for FUN is GVO
what is the code for SMILE?

TNHKD

If the code for SAD is RZC,
what is the code for HAPPY?

IBQQZ

If the code for WARM is XBSN,
what does DPME mean?

COLD

If the code for CARS is BZQR,
what does UZMR mean?

WANT

? Puzzle Pointer

Find the pattern between the
first letter of the word and the
first letter of the code then copy
the pattern:

CAT has the code DBU so what
is the code for OWL?

C to D is + 1 so O + 1 is P

A to B is + 1 so W + 1 is X

T to U is + 1 so L + 1 is M

The answer is PXM.

19

Warm-up

Six horses have to return to their stables. Write the name of the correct horse in each stable. Use the clues to help you.

- Sugar is a sweet horse who is between her two best friends Dollar and Honey and opposite Bella.

- Merry is opposite Honey and next to Vinny.

- Bella is in stable 4 and further left than Vinny.

1	2	3	
Dollar	Sugar	Honey	
4	5	6
Bella	Merry	Vinny

Puzzle Pointer

Put the initials of the horses that could fit into each stable and then add more or cross them out as you read through the rest of the clues.

16 Sugar cubes 1

Owen is working out how much sugar is in his favourite foods. How many cubes are there?

7 cubes of sugar

13 cubes of sugar

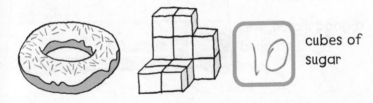

10 cubes of sugar

17 Building sandcastles 1

Add one letter each time to make a new word. Use the clues to help you.

b e t	rhymes with let
b e a t	a steady rhythm
b e a s t	a wild animal
b r e a s t	the red part of a robin

to use a chair

a jacket and trousers set

a sofa and chairs set

a good match, well matched

i t
s i t
s u i t
s u i t e
s u i t e d

22

owns

they keep
heads warm

talks casually

breaks the rules

foot digit

past tense of tear

a shop

packed away

Puzzle Pointer

If you can't work out a word, move on to the next one, and then go back to it.

23

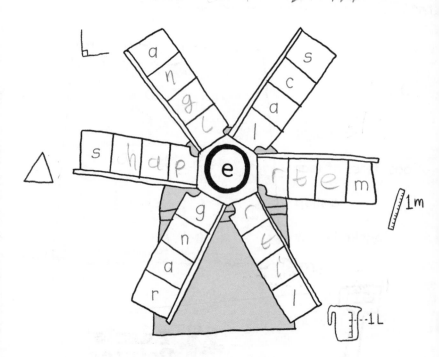

Warm-up

Put all of these letters into the correct place on the windmill to find six words we use in maths. All the words start from the outside so some will be written backwards. The first letter of each word is given and they all end in **e**. There are picture clues to help you. Two have been done for you.

a d d a c e e g g h i l l m n n p r r r t t s s

Puzzle Pointer

Cross out the letters as you use them to make it easier to see which letters are left over.

24

Warm-up

19 Meerkat meeting

The meerkats are in a meeting. Work out where they are each sitting. Write the name of the correct meerkat on each place.

- Brains, Cyril, Dave and Timid sit in corner seats.
- Lofty is next to Brains and Mini and is opposite Vicious who is next to Spike and Cyril.
- Mini is in seat 3 and opposite Spike.
- Timid is sitting in an even numbered seat.

1 Brains	2 Lofty	3 Mini	4 Timid
8 Cyril	7 Vicious	6 Spike	5 Dave

Here are the names and dates of birth of five school friends. Use the information to solve the puzzle below.

Baahir: 13 August 2008   Rosie: 24 June 2009

Elliot: 29 February 2008   Cade: 8 January 2008

Lydia: 23 November 2009

The first letter of the oldest child

The last letter of the second youngest child

The first letter of the youngest child

The last letter of the oldest child

The first letter of the child who has the middle age

The last letter of the child with a summer holiday birthday

The last letter of the child with an autumn birthday

The last letter of the child with a birthday every four years

The first letter of the child who is the second oldest

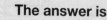

The answer is

.

 Sudoku images 1

Look at these images:

Complete the grid by placing the nine images so that:

- each row has only one of each image
- each column has only one of each image
- each block of nine has only one of each image.

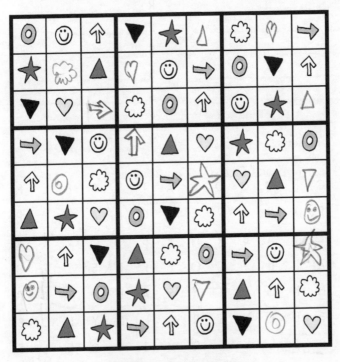

 **Puzzle Pointer**

Look for rows, columns or blocks with only one empty
square, and try to work out what shape is missing.

22 Colour names

Hidden in the word search are 20 colours that are named after food, drinks, plants, metals or gemstones. The first letter of each colour and the number of letters is given as a clue.

C h e r r y   M i n t
C h o c o l a t e   O _ _ _ _ _
C o f f e e   P e a c h
C r e a m   R a s p b e r r y
E _ _ _ _ _ _   R u b y
G o l d   S a g e
L _ _ _ _ _ _ _   S i l v e r
L _ _ _ _ _   S a p p h i r e
L _ _ _ _   S a l m o n
L i m e   V e n d e r

C	H	O	C	O	L	A	T	E	S	E	L	M
R	X	R	Z	P	E	A	C	H	A	O	A	R
E	V	A	B	R	M	E	B	G	G	V	V	A
A	H	N	J	C	O	F	F	E	E	I	E	S
M	K	G	R	T	N	S	A	L	M	O	N	P
F	L	E	M	E	R	A	L	D	Y	L	D	B
S	I	L	V	E	R	M	I	V	C	E	E	E
E	L	E	G	O	L	D	M	I	N	T	R	R
S	A	P	P	H	I	R	E	L	O	Y	Y	R
P	C	R	R	U	B	Y	C	H	E	R	R	Y

28

23 Say what you see 1

Find the five names hidden here by solving
this sound puzzle. If you say them out loud,
do they sound like letters?

1. Are oh bee   _R ob_

2. Jay oh why   _Joy_

3. Are ay why   _Ray_

4. Kay ay tea why   _Katy_

5. Bee ay are are why   _Barry_

Find the five animal names hidden here using the clues.

1. D 👂   _Deer_

2. c @   _Cat_

3. E L E 🌀 T   _Elephant_

4. D O N 🗝   _Donkey_

5. 〰 L   _Seal_

Puzzle Pointer

The pictures will help you with how the names of the
animals sound but not with the spellings! Take care
to write the correct spelling in the answer words.

24 Find the trapeziums

Find the 17 trapeziums hidden in the picture below.

(25) Pick the lock 1

Here are four keys and four locks. Draw a line to match each key to the right lock.

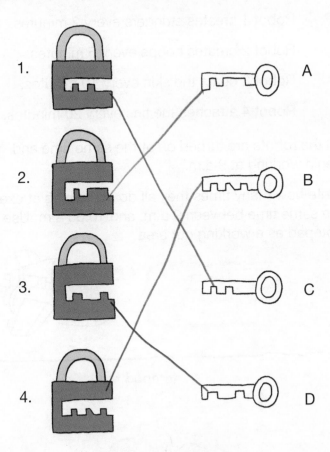

1.   A

2.   B

3.   C

4.   D

Puzzle Pointer

Look carefully at where the longest prongs are as this will match up with the lowest dips in the lock.

(26) It is rocket science!

These four robots are all doing an important job building prototype space rockets.

- Robot 1 creates stringers every 2 minutes.

- Robot 2 creates hoops every 5 minutes.

- Robot 3 coats the skin every 10 minutes.

- Robot 4 attaches the fins every 20 minutes.

All the robots are turned on at the same time and begin working at 9 a.m.

Write how many times they all do something at exactly the same time between 9 a.m. and 10.05 a.m. Use the notepad as a working out area.

Notepad

27 Corner conundrum 1

Four children have drawn some tiles, but one corner of each tile is missing. Fill in the missing corner to complete the pattern on each tile.

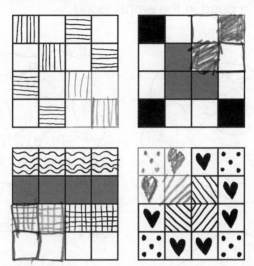

One corner of this tile is missing. Fill in the missing corner to complete the pattern.

Instead of five ponds with four fish in each, there are four ponds with five fish. Look closely at the meaning of the words, then write the odd one out from each pond in the empty pond.

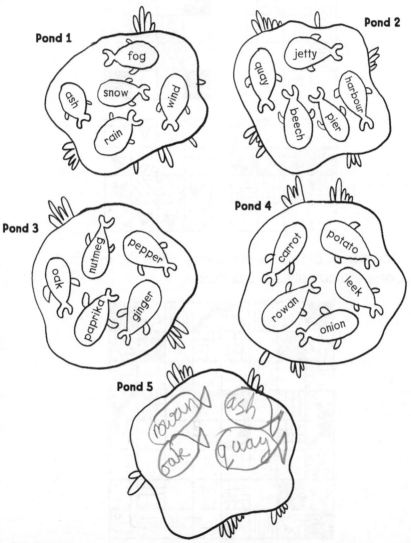

Pond 1
fog, ash, snow, wind, rain

Pond 2
jetty, quay, beech, pier, harbour

Pond 3
nutmeg, pepper, oak, paprika, ginger

Pond 4
carrot, potato, leek, rowan, onion

Pond 5
rowan, ash, oak, quay

34

29 Word sandwiches 1

A café is selling four new word sandwiches. To make a sandwich there is a word on the top, in the filling, in the salad and on the bottom. One letter is changed each time to make four words for example, **plan**, **flan**, **flap**, **clap**.

There are clues to each word next to each sandwich.

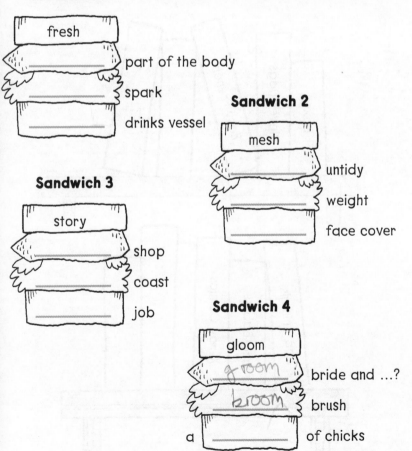

Sandwich 1

fresh

_____ part of the body

_____ spark

_____ drinks vessel

Sandwich 2

mesh

_____ untidy

_____ weight

_____ face cover

Sandwich 3

story

_____ shop

_____ coast

_____ job

Sandwich 4

gloom

groom bride and ...?

broom brush

a _____ of chicks

Warm-up

Nish's bookshelf needs tidying up. Every book should be in order and every shelf has a different order.

Work out the pattern, then make up your own book titles that continue the pattern. The first letter of each book title forms a sequence and the first letter of the second word also forms a sequence. Use the alphabet to help you.

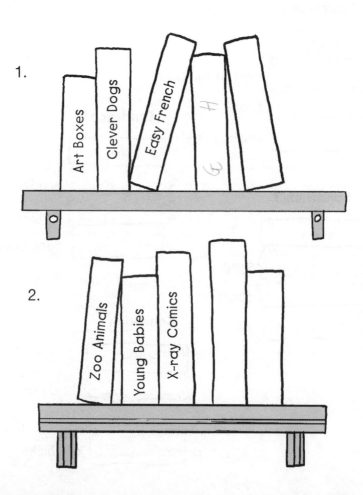

1. Art Boxes | Clever Dogs | Easy French | H | G

2. Zoo Animals | Young Babies | X-ray Comics

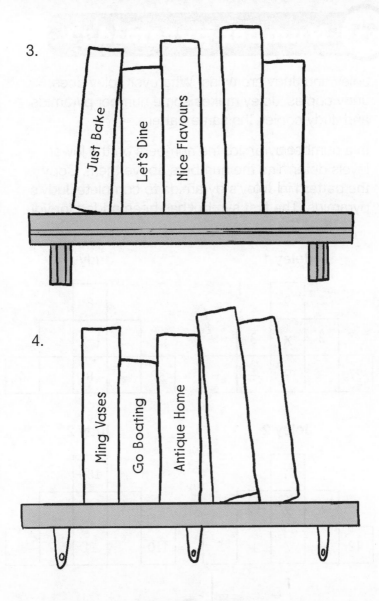

3.

Just Bake

Let's Dine

Nice Flavours

4.

Ming Vases

Go Boating

Antique Home

ABCDEFGHIJKLMNOPQRSTUVWXYZ

31 Number pyramids 1

Joley and Judy are twins. Whatever Joley does, Judy copies. Joley makes some number pyramids and Judy copies the same pattern.

In a number pyramid, the numbers on the lower levels determine the numbers above them. Copy the pattern in Joley's pyramids to complete Judy's pyramids. The first symbol has been added for you.

Joley 1

		9		
	3	×	3	
27	÷	9	÷	3

Judy 1

		8		
32	÷	8		4

Joley 2

		72		
	6	×	12	
42	÷	7	+	5

Judy 2

		180		
110		11		

Puzzle Pointer

Copy the symbols across and then work out the sums to find the number in the square above.

There are two pieces missing from the puzzle but eight pieces to choose from.

Circle the right pieces to complete the puzzle and draw a line to which section they belong in.

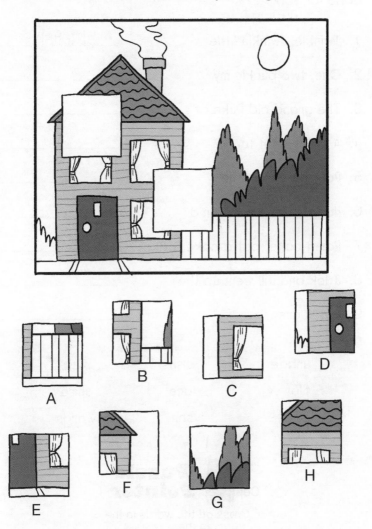

A

B

C

D

E

F

G

H

Warm-up

Here are the first lines of some well-known rhymes and songs. The last word is missing. Write the missing word and add one of the words from the box below to make a new word. The first one has been done for you.

1. Twinkle, twinkle little _____starfish_____

2. One, two buckle my _____

3. The grand old Duke of _____

4. A sailor went to _____

5. Polly put the kettle _____

6. Humpty Dumpty sat on a _____

7. Pat-a-cake, pat-a-cake, baker's _____

8. Jack and Jill went up the _____

9. Roses are _____

made	dish	~~fish~~
flower	lace	shire
side	son	wards

Puzzle Pointer

Cross off the words in the box as you use them.

34 Spot the difference

There are nine differences between the two pictures.
See if you can find them all.

41

35 Dotty dominoes 1

Look at the dominoes and use them to answer the questions below.

1. How many dominoes have an odd number of dots?

2. How many dominoes have the same number of dots on both sides?

3. Subtract the second answer from the first answer.

4. Draw this number of dots in four different ways on the dominoes below.

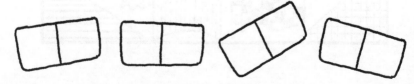

36 Paper snowflakes 1

Tyler has folded some paper and then cut out some shapes. Draw what you would see each time when Tyler opens up the paper. The first one has been done for you.

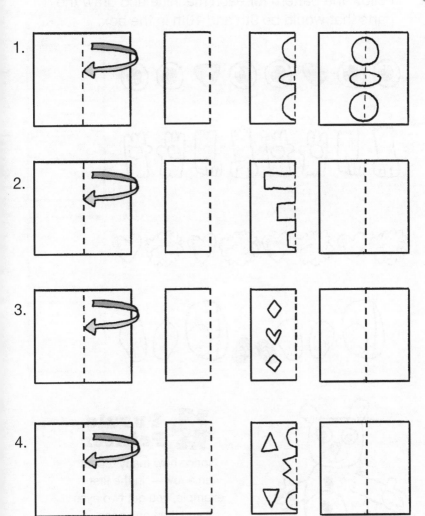

(37) Production line 1

There are four machines in a factory all cutting out shapes to make teddy bears. Here are the first eight parts made by each machine.

Follow the pattern for each machine and draw the parts that would be 9th and 10th in the box.

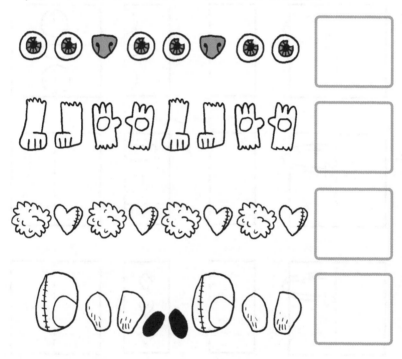

Puzzle Pointer

Notice how many repeat in a row — in the first example, you get two eyes and then one nose.

38 Transformers

Look at how the picture on the top has changed and choose the picture that copies the same change.

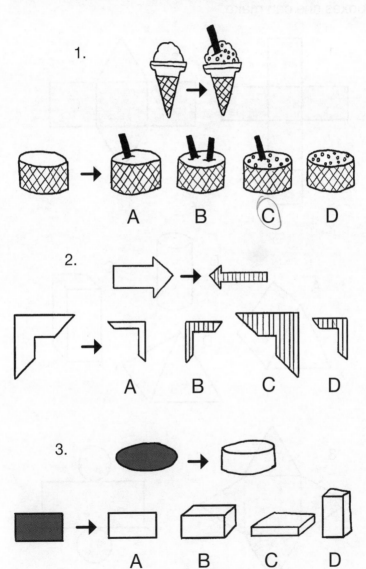

1.

A B C D

2.

A B C D

3.

A B C D

39 Gift wrapping

Olivia needs to wrap some gifts. Join the flat, grey shapes to the correct 3D shapes to show her what boxes she can make.

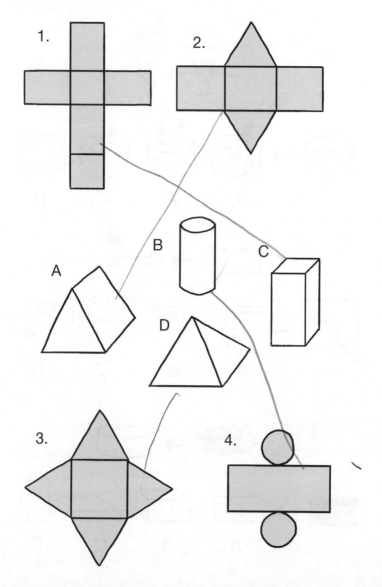

1.

2.

A

B

C

D

3.

4.

46

40 Pairs 2

Every shape here has an exact match except for one.

Circle the one shape that does not have a matching pair.

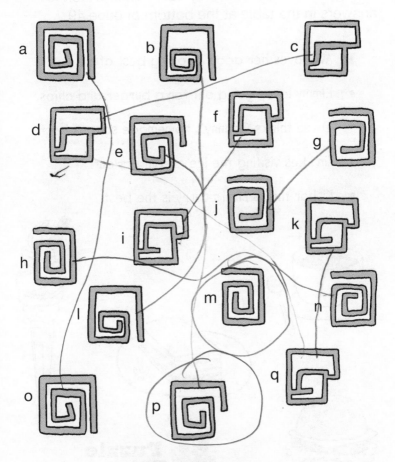

a b c

d f

e g

j

i k

h

l m n

q

o p

? Puzzle Pointer

When you spot a matching pair cross out both shapes.

41 Food favourites

Five children have been asked to name their favourite food and who makes it. They all choose a different favourite food. Use the clues to find out who enjoys eating what and where they eat it. Then write the answers in the table at the bottom of page 49.

- Ava loves her dad's cooking best of all.

- Kimmy loves going out for a burger and chips.

- Owen thinks Granny's homemade soup is best.

- Fin likes visiting the ice cream parlour.

- Kishor thinks Mimi's curry is the best.

Puzzle Pointer

Add ticks and crosses to the chart at the top of page 49 for the answers you know. Then work out where to put the remaining ticks.

	Granny's house	Mimi's house	Dad's house	Mr Burger	Nice Ices	Burger	Curry	Ice cream	Lasagne	Soup
Ava										
Kishor										
Fin										
Kimmy										
Owen										
Burger					
Curry					
Ice cream					
Lasagne					
Soup					

Child	Food	Place
Ava		
Kishor		
Fin		
Kimmy		
Owen		

Puzzle power!

How did you do? Check the answers at the end of the book and add up how many warm-up puzzles you got right. Score 2 for each fully correct puzzle, and 1 if you got some of the puzzle right. Write down your total and read on to discover your puzzle power...

My puzzle power score is

Puzzle power score 1–25

Great start! Your puzzle power has begun to grow. Why don't you take another look at some of the puzzles you weren't sure about before heading to the next section?

Puzzle power score 26–49

Well done! Your puzzle power is blossoming and you're getting warmed up for the intermediate puzzles.

Puzzle power score 50+

You have brilliant puzzle power! You are ready to zoom straight to the intermediate puzzles and take on some more puzzle challenges.

Intermediate
puzzles

42 Picture codes

Here are some shapes with a code underneath. Work out which part of the shape matches which part of the code and use this to write the code for the final shape.

Code 1

A L W   B M X   A M Y   B N W   _ _ _

Code 2

S K D   S L E   T K F   U M D   _ _ _

Code 3

N U T   O V S   P W T   N V T   _ _ _

Puzzle Pointer

Look for two codes with the same letters and see which parts of the drawings are the same.

52

Look at the code and work out the secret message. This time there is one code for two letters to make this even trickier. Good luck!

!	?	#	@	*	£	&	+	=	%	^	/	:
A	B	C	D	E	F	G	H	I	J	K	L	M
N	O	P	Q	R	S	T	U	V	W	X	Y	Z

%	*	=	&	=	!	&
W	R	I	T	I	N	G

=	!
I	N

£	*	#	*	*	&
S	E	C	R	E	T

#	?	@	*
C	O	D	E

=	£
I	S

!
A

&	*	*	!	&
G	R	E	A	T

%	!	/
W	A	Y

?	£
O	F

£	*	!	@	=	!	&
S	E	N	D	I	N	G

:	*	£	£	!	&	*	£
M	E	S	S	A	G	E	S

#	*	*	!	&	*
C	R	E	A	T	E

/	?	+	*
Y	O	U	R

?	%	!
O	W	N

£	*	#	*	*	&
S	E	C	R	E	T

#	?	@	*	£
C	O	D	E	?

&	?
T	O

#	+	!	/	/	*	!	&	*
C	H	A	L	L	E	N	G	E

/	?	+	*
Y	O	U	R

£	*	=	*	!	@	£
F	R	I	E	N	D	S

44 Mixed messages 2

There are two mixed up sentences here. Work out what they both say and where the spaces between the words should be.

Intermediate

TTohreenswoelnve
eetdhtioswwoernk
eoeudttwohwerriet
tehoeustpeavceers
ysohtohuelrdlgeot
ttoemratkoemsaek
nesoeuorfttwhoess
eenntteennccees.

_____

_____

_____

_____

_____

_____

45 Pattern popping

These shapes always follow in the same order to make a pattern. Two of the shapes have swapped places. Can you find which ones they are and circle them?

55

The owl has pinched the vowels again! Rewrite these words to make 12 well-known vegetables.

Intermediate

1. p t t _____

2. c r r t _____

3. p r s n p _____

4. l k _____

5. n n _____

6. c b b g _____

7. c l f l w r _____

8. b r c c l _____

9. s p n c h _____

10. b n _____

11. s w t c r n _____

12. s p r t _____

Puzzle Pointer

One word begins with a vowel.

47 Boxes

Here is a grid 64 squares in area. Divide the grid into four so that each shape has exactly the same area **but** is a different shape from the others. You can't draw a line through the middle of any of the square.

 Puzzle Pointer

 First, work out how many squares each shape needs to cover for them all to have the same area.

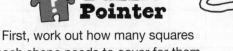

(48) Park path

The park needs a path that leads from the top to the bottom following these rules:

- The path needs to be one square wide.
- There must be at least one square between the path and a tree or water.
- The path must move horizontally and vertically, not diagonally, and must use only 13 squares.

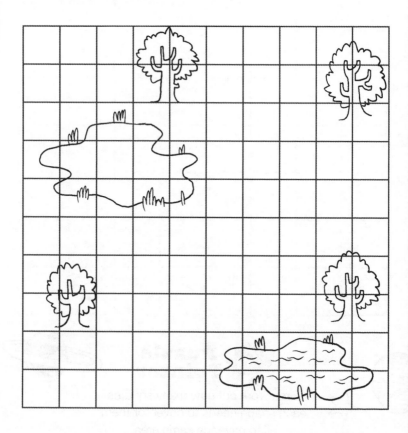

49 Puzzle pairs 1

There are four pairs of identical puzzle pieces hidden in the box below. Draw lines to join the four pairs together.

 **Puzzle Pointer**

Watch out! Not all the pieces have pairs.

50 Shipping lanes

On page 61, there are lots of boats that all need to manoeuvre into the right place.

A large ship is made from four shaded squares.

Place the ten large ships.

A yacht is made from three shaded squares.

Place the ten yachts.

A small rowing boat is made from two shaded squares.

Place the ten small rowing boats.

Rules

- Every shaded square in the grid opposite is part of a boat

- Every shaded square needs to be drawn around to make a ship, yacht or rowing boat.

- Each boat can be diagonal, vertical or horizontal but always in a straight line.

- No shaded squares can be shared.

A yacht and a rowing boat have been circled for you.

Puzzle Pointer

Cross off each boat as you circle its position in the grid.

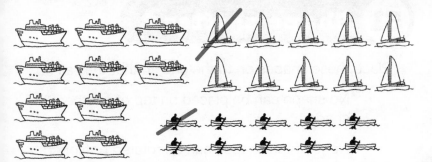

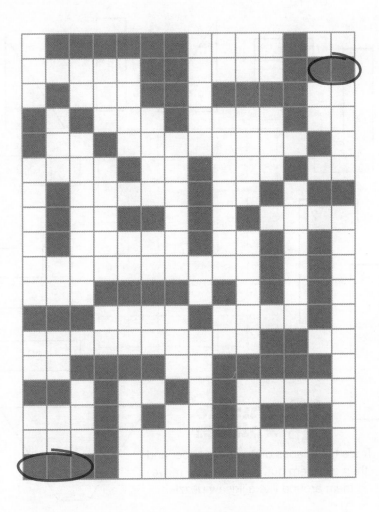

61

Place these shapes on to the grid so that they all fit.

- No shape can be placed on top of another shape.

- None of the shapes can be rotated or flipped over.

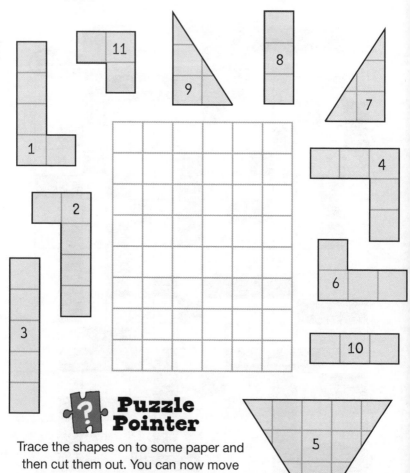

Puzzle Pointer

Trace the shapes on to some paper and then cut them out. You can now move them around like a jigsaw puzzle.

52 Riddle and rhyme 2

Solve the clues to find the missing word. Use the notepad as a working out area.

My first letter is in **frost** and also in **snow**, ———

My second is in **ice** but not in **window**. ———

My third is in **favourite** and in **holiday**, ———

My fourth is in **slush** and also in **sleigh**. ———

My fifth is in **snowball** and also in **cold**, ———

My sixth is in **young** but it isn't in **old**. ———

My whole lasts for months, can you find the reason?

An example is 'winter', my word is ——————— .

Intermediate

Notepad

A B C D E F G H I J K L M N O P Q R S T U V W X Y Z

If the code for BERRY is YVIIB,
what is the code for HOLLY?   _____

If the code for FUNNY is UFMMB,
what is the code for COMEDY?   _____

If the code for WEALTHY is DVZOGSB
what does KIVXRLFH mean?   _____

If the code for TRICKY is GIRXPB,
what does WRUURXFOG mean?   _____

Puzzle Pointer

Look at the position of the letter
and its code on the alphabet line.
What do you notice?

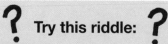

Try this riddle:

If you are clever enough to solve these codes, try
solving this. What has 50 heads and 50 tails but no
body, hands or feet?

54 Map matching

Perry has a map on his phone. He is trying to find Trampoline World. Which building is Trampoline World? Circle it.

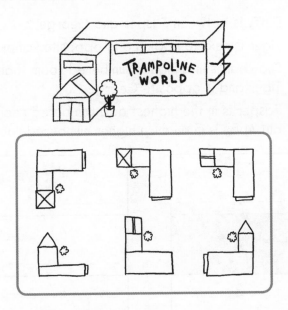

After Trampoline World, Perry visits Perfect Pizza. Here is the restaurant:

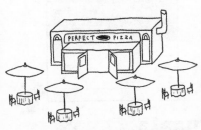

Can you draw the restaurant as it would look on Perry's map?

Intermediate

The Kitten Hotel has eight rooms for the kittens to sleep in. Use the clues to work out where each kitten will be.

- Fluffy is between Jasper and George.
- Tiger is next to Bodkin and opposite Pumpkin.
- Snowball is in a higher numbered room than Tiger and is opposite George.
- Jasper is in the highest odd numbered room, but Abby is in an even higher numbered room.

1 _____	2 _____
	4 _____
3 _____	6 _____
5 _____	
7 _____	8 _____

? Puzzle Pointer

Make sure you read all the clues first before you start to work out who is where. You might find it easier not to work through them in order.

56 Building sandcastles 2

Add one letter each time to make a new word. You can move the letters around. There are clues to help.

1.

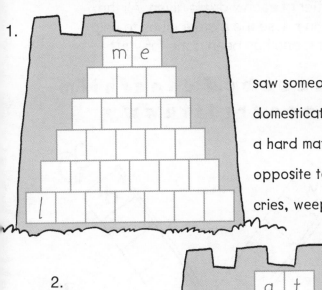

| m | e |

| l | | | | | |

saw someone

domesticated like a pet

a hard material

opposite to physical

cries, weeps

2.

headwear

a questioning word

anger

a circle of flowers

sunny, rainy, snowy?

| a | t |

| w |

Puzzle Pointer

If you find the clue 'anger' tricky, try using a thesaurus to help you.

57 Windmill words 2

Put these letters into the correct place on the windmill to find six jobs that people do.
The first letter of each word is given. All the words end in **r**. Use the picture clues to help you. The first one has been done for you.

~~a~~ ~~a~~ a a a ~~b~~ b c ~~d~~ ~~e~~ e e e ~~f~~ h i ~~l~~ m
o o o ~~r~~ r r t t t u ~~w~~ ~~w~~ ~~y~~

58 Divide and rule

The farmer has to place her sheep into four fields. Each field needs one shed for shelter, one water trough for drinking and five sheep. Use only two straight lines to divide the area up in the right way.

59 Football fun

It's the end of the football season. Use the clues to put the football teams in order from first to last.

- Chelsea is only lower than two teams and Nottingham Forest is only higher than two teams.

- Manchester City is one place higher than Liverpool and two places lower than Everton.

- Swansea City did better than Wolverhampton Wanderers but not as well as Everton.

- Sunderland beat Southampton but Nottingham Forest and Tranmere Rovers beat Sunderland.

 **Puzzle Pointer**

Read through all the clues at least once before you start trying to work out the order.

1st _____

2nd _____

3rd _____

4th _____

5th _____

6th _____

7th _____

8th _____

9th _____

10th _____

Sudoku images 2

Look at these images:

Complete the grid by placing each of the nine images so that:

- each row has only one of each image
- each column has only one of each image
- each block of nine has only one of each image.

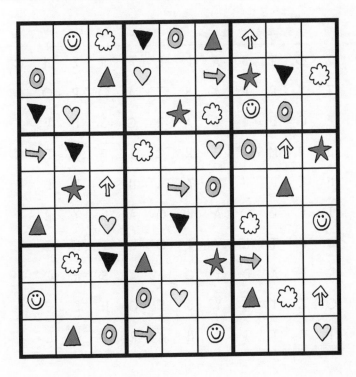

Hidden in the word search are five types of sport, language, food, instrument and book. Find the words and put them into their correct categories.

Sport	Language	Food	Instrument	Book

Intermediate

F	O	O	T	B	A	L	L	F	R	E	N	C	H
L	T	V	R	P	A	S	T	A	O	R	O	R	C
U	E	G	U	I	T	A	R	C	S	U	V	I	H
T	N	R	M	A	G	R	C	T	P	G	E	C	I
E	N	E	P	N	R	A	A	U	A	B	L	K	N
B	I	E	E	O	A	B	G	A	N	Y	R	E	E
U	S	K	T	L	V	I	O	L	I	N	I	T	S
B	R	E	A	D	Y	C	L	A	S	R	C	Y	E
P	O	E	T	R	Y	S	F	C	H	E	E	S	E
D	I	C	T	I	O	N	A	R	Y	P	L	A	Y

62 3D printing

James has a 3D printer so whatever he draws in 2D, he can print out in 3D. Here are some of his drawings. Match the 3D print out to the drawings but be careful, there are some extra pictures here to try and trick you!

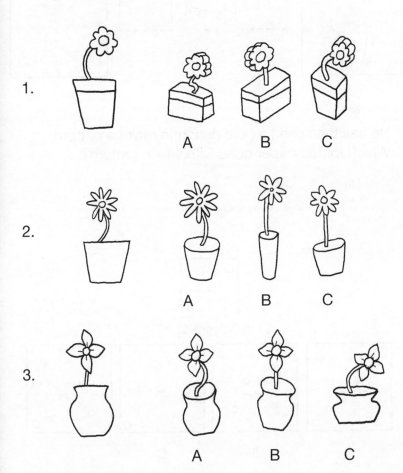

1.

A   B   C

2.

A   B   C

3.

A   B   C

Mohammed has folded up four sheets of paper into quarters like this:

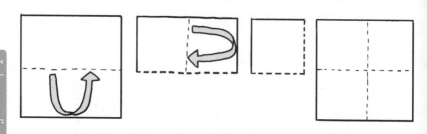

He has then used a hole punch to make a pattern. Which folded paper goes with which pattern?

1.

Pattern 1

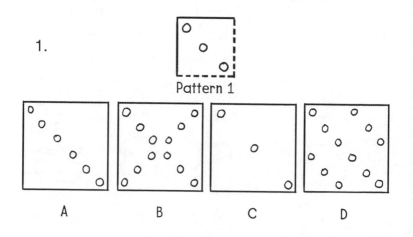

A   B   C   D

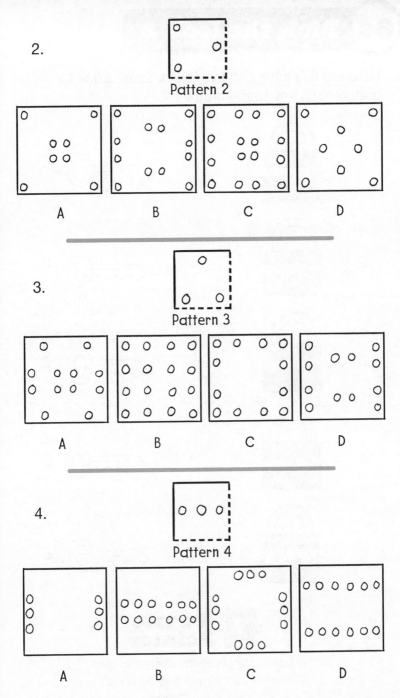

2.

Pattern 2

A   B   C   D

3.

Pattern 3

A   B   C   D

4.

Pattern 4

A   B   C   D

64 Pick the lock 2

Here are five keys and five locks. Draw a line to match each key to the right lock.

1.

 A

2.

 B

3.

 C

4.

 D

5.

 E

Puzzle Pointer

Look carefully at the shapes of the prongs as they will match up with the dips in the lock.

Intermediate

All of the stars need to be in groups of six. Each star can only be in one group and there must be one black star and one grey star burst in every group. Draw circles round the groups of stars.

66 Corner conundrum 2

Four children have drawn some tiles, but one corner of each tile is missing. Fill in the missing corner so that the patterns on the tiles are complete.

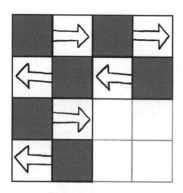

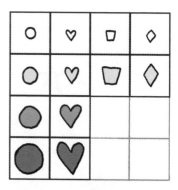

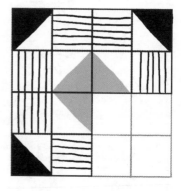

67 Missing half

Half of this tile is missing. Draw the missing half so it looks symmetrical.

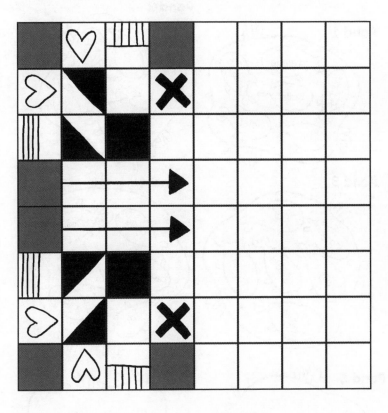

Find a picture of a person's face in an old magazine. Fold the picture exactly in half so that you see half of the face. Now try drawing the missing half of the person.

Choose two fish from each pond that need to be moved into the empty ponds.

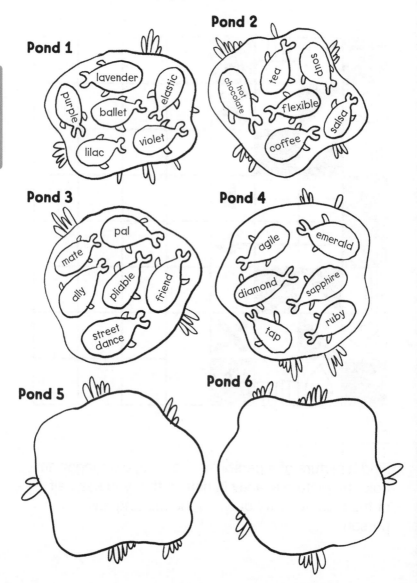

Pond 2

Pond 1

lavender
purple
ballet
elastic
lilac
violet

hot chocolate
tea
soup
flexible
salsa
coffee

Pond 3

Pond 4

pal
mate
ally
pliable
friend
street dance

agile
emerald
diamond
sapphire
tap
ruby

Pond 5

Pond 6

Intermediate

69 Word sandwiches 2

A café is selling four new word sandwiches. To make a sandwich there is a word on the top, one in the filling, one in the salad and another on the bottom. One letter is changed each time to make four words for example, **plan**, **flan**, **flap**, **clap**.

Sandwich 1

chops

_____ stores

_____ boats

_____ falls over

Sandwich 2

plump

_____ to collapse

_____ a short stub

_____ on a letter

Sandwich 3

clown

_____ royal symbol

_____ big, black birds

_____ above the eyes

Sandwich 4

toaster

_____ cooked bread (verb)

_____ oven cooked

_____ nested

Puzzle Pointer

There are clues to each word next to the sandwich.

70 Book building 2

Jasmine's bookshelf needs tidying up. Every book should be in order and every shelf has a different order.

Work out the pattern, then make up your own book titles that continue the pattern. The first letter of each book title forms a sequence and the first letter of the second word also forms a sequence. Use the alphabet to help you.

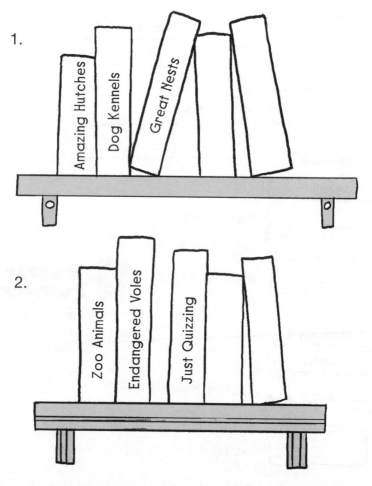

1.

Amazing Hutches · Dog Kennels · Great Nests

2.

Zoo Animals · Endangered Voles · Just Quizzing

3.

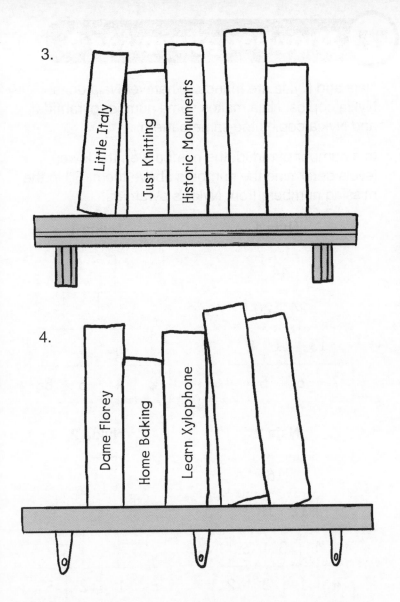

Little Italy

Just Knitting

Historic Monuments

4.

Dame Florey

Home Baking

Learn Xylophone

ABCDEFGHIJKLMNOPQRSTUVWXYZ

71 Number pyramids 2

Naja and Nykia are friends. Whatever Naja does, Nykia copies. Naja makes some number pyramids and Nykia copies the same pattern.

In a number pyramid, the numbers on the lower levels determine the numbers above them. Fill in the missing numbers from Nykia's pyramids.

Naja 1

Nykia 1

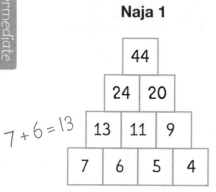

$7 + 6 = 13$

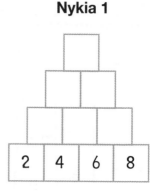

Naja 2

Nykia 2

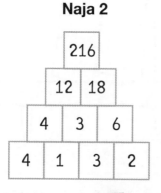

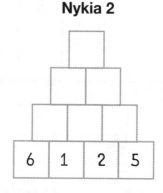

Puzzle Pointer

This time the number pyramids don't include symbols. You could write the symbols between each number on Naja's pyramids to help you.

72 Rhyme plus one 2

Here are the first lines from some well-known rhymes and songs. The last word is missing. Write the missing word and add one of the words from the box below to make a new word. The first one has been done for you.

1. Jack be nimble, Jack be ___quicksand___

2. Lavender's _____

3. London Bridge is falling _____

4. Row, row, row your _____

5. Old McDonald had a _____

6. Have you seen the muffin _____

7. Wind the bobbin _____

8. The wheels on the _____

9. Baa Baa black _____

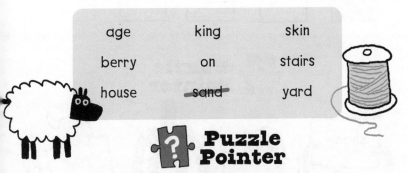

age	king	skin
berry	on	stairs
house	~~sand~~	yard

？ Puzzle Pointer

Once you have worked out the missing word, try putting each word in the box before it and after it to see if it makes a new word.

Draw what will come next in the box.

Pattern 1

Pattern 2

Pattern 3

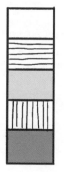 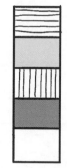 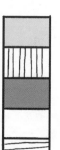  

Puzzle Pointer

shade

shape

direction

size

74 Dotty dominoes 2

Look at the dominoes and use them to answer the questions below.

1. How many dominoes have more than 8 dots? ⬚

2. How many dominoes have fewer than 6 dots? ⬚

3. Subtract the first answer from the second answer. ⬚

4. Draw this number of dots in three different ways on the dominoes below.

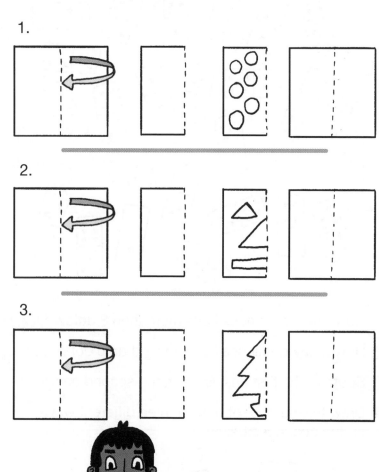

Ajay has folded some paper and then cut out some shapes. Draw what you would see when Ajay opens up the paper.

1.

2.

3.

Intermediate

There are four machines in the factory all making food.

Follow the pattern for each machine and draw the item that would be the 20th on the line in the box.

Intermediate

Here are some sentences but they don't look like they should. Can you still work out what the sentences say?

We get so used
to seeing words in just
one direction.

But this shows you just how clever your brain is to still make sense of it.

If you can read it, you must have a genius brain!

(78) Craft creation

Here is a brilliant way of making a flat piece of paper into a 3D tray to store little things in.

1. Take one piece of square paper (any size you like).

2. Fold two corners together to make a triangle shape. Unfold and do the same in the other direction so that you can find the centre.

3. Fold the four corners of the square into the centre.

4. Now you have a smaller square, fold the four new corners into the centre.

5. Take the point of each of these corners and fold it backwards so the tip touches the outside edge of the square.

6. In the middle you can see the corners of your original square. Take each one and fold it backwards so that it forms an upright triangle.

7. Ta da! You now have a mini tray.

Intermediate

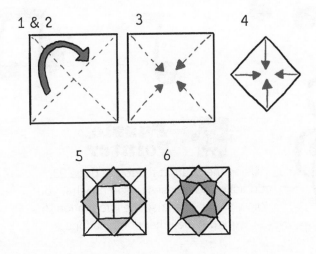

It's the grand final of the dancing competition and each dancer has a partner and a dance routine. Use the clues to find out which dancers are together and the dances they are performing. Then write the answers in the table at the bottom of page 93.

- Parva loves his cha cha cha, but not with Zuri.
- Enya is dancing with Tom.
- Harry is dancing a foxtrot but not with Zuri or Amy.
- Bella loves the waltz, but not with Marco.
- Neither Amy nor Enya are dancing the salsa.
- Tom is dancing the jive.

Puzzle Pointer

Using the chart at the top of page 93, add ticks and crosses based on what you know so far. Then use the information to work out the other combinations.

Intermediate

	Cha cha cha	Foxtrot	Jive	Salsa	Waltz	Angelo	Harry	Marco	Parva	Tom
Amy										
Bella										
Enya										
Zuri										
Lian										
Angelo										
Harry										
Marco										
Parva										
Tom										

Dancer	Dance	Partner
Amy		
Bella		
Enya		
Zuri		
Lian		

Puzzle power!

Is your puzzle power building as you do more puzzles? Check the answers at the end of the book and add up how many puzzles you got right. Score 2 for each fully correct puzzle, and 1 if you got some of the puzzle right. Write down your total and see if your puzzle power is growing.

My puzzle power score is

Puzzle power score 1-25

Great work! Your puzzle power has continued to grow. Look back over at some of the puzzles before leaping on to the tricky puzzles.

Puzzle power score 26-49

Well done! Your puzzle power is growing and you're getting warmed up for the tricky puzzles.

Puzzle power score 50+

You are bursting with puzzle power! You are ready to rocket straight to the tricky puzzles and tackle even more puzzle challenges.

Tricky
puzzles

80 Alien codes

Work out which part of the alien matches which part of the code. Use this to write the code for the final shape.

Code 1

AJP   BKQ   ALR   BLP

Code 2

SJG   SKH   TKF   TJH

Code 3

ZDL   YEM   YFN   XFL

Tricky

Look at the code and work out the secret message.

1	2	3	4	5	6	7	8	9
A	D	G	J	M	P	S	V	Y
B	E	H	K	N	Q	T	W	Z
C	F	I	L	O	R	U	X	

1	1	5

9	5	7

7	7	2

9	5	7	6

6	5	8	2	6	7

5	2

4	5	3	3	1

7	5

7	5	4	8	2

7	3	3	7

7	2	1	6	2	7

1	5	2	2	?

97

There are six entries for the kitty competition this year: Boo Boo, Joe, Peaches, Snowdrop, Fifi and Colin. They are all wearing different colour collars. Follow the clues to solve the problem and then answer the questions below.

- Boo Boo has a collar with a tag, but no bell, unlike Peaches who has a bell but no tag. Neither have a blue or yellow collar.

- Fifi and Snowdrop have a bell and a tag but neither is wearing a blue or silver collar.

- Peaches is not wearing the pink or silver collar and neither is Colin who does have a tag and bell, and who is wearing a green collar.

- Joe has no tag, no bell but his collar is blue.

- Fifi loves her pink collar.

- One cat is wearing a red collar.

Tricky

98

	Colour	Tag	Bell
Boo Boo			
Joe			
Peaches			
Snowdrop			
Fifi			
Colin			

How many cats have both a tag and a bell?

How many cats have neither a tag nor a bell?

The winner of the competition had a yellow collar, a tag and a bell.

Who was the winner?

83 18s

Draw a circle around groups of numbers that total 18.

- You can't use a number more than once.

- Every number needs to be used.

- A group can be any size as long as every number inside adds up to 18.

- You can make a group horizontally, vertically or diagonally.

One has been done for you.

1	8	4	2	4	3	4	5	6	2
5	7	3	6	6	8	3	4	4	3
4	5	4	9	3	3	5	3	5	4
5	5	3	8	6	6	2	9	4	5
9	7	5	1	1	2	3	2	5	4
2	6	7	7	5	3	3	9	9	5
6	6	3	3	9	6	3	3	6	7
2	2	4	4	6	3	3	3	9	9

84 Mixed messages 3

Did you know that your brain has the power to solve words that are in the strangest of formats? Read these sentences and see if your brain can make sense of them.

> 50met1me5 0ur bra1n w1ll make 5en5e 0f w0rd5 w1th number5 1n them t0 replace 50me letter5.
>
> Somtims th sntencs mght b mssng sme of th lttrs nd stll our brn cn mke snse of them.
>
> E^en $tr%nger is wh8n our br8in ta£e$ the rea""y b1za99e c0mb1nat1on o£ letter$, numb&r$ and $ymb0l$ and $t1ll, we c)n mana9e to m(ke $ense of 1t.

Tricky

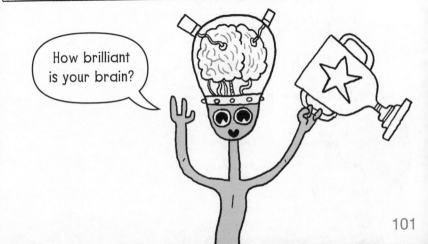

How brilliant is your brain?

101

The owl has pinched the vowels again! Insert the vowels to make the names of 14 sports.

1. f t b l l _____

2. b s b l l _____

3. b s k t b l l _____

4. r n d r s _____

5. t n n s _____

6. c r c k t _____

7. s n k r _____

8. h c k y _____

9. s w m m n g _____

10. b d m n t n _____

11. s c b d v n g _____

12. r w n g _____

13. h r s r d n g _____

14. r c h r y _____

Tricky

VOWELS

86 Say what you see 2

Use the symbols and sounds to unlock the message. Some are famous sayings; some need you to say what you see!

1.

| More Not More More Not More | it = difficult difficult | See See |  |

<u>More often than not it is too difficult</u>

<u>to see the bigger picture.</u>

2.

 is | tricky tricky | people people people people |

_____

_____

3.

Erm? I wonder | THIS = funny funny | words words words words

_____

_____

Puzzle Pointer

These puzzles will test your brain power! Look at the how many times a word is repeated. This will help you unlock the message.

Tricky

Place these shapes on to the grid so that they all fit.

- No shape can fit on top of another shape.
- None of the shapes can be be rotated or flipped over.

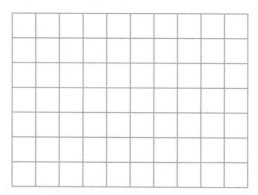

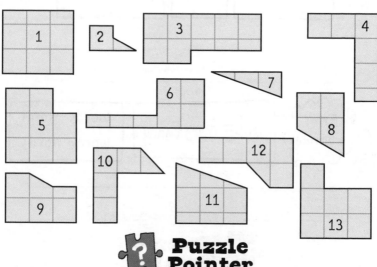

Puzzle Pointer

Trace the shapes on to paper and then cut them out. You can then place them in different positions until you find the right fit.

A B C D E F G H I J K L M N O P Q R S T U V W X Y Z

If the code for MUSIC is LTRHB,
what is the code for RADIO?

_____

If the code for ORANGE is PSBOHF,
what is the code for PURPLE?

_____

If the code for BANQUET is
DZRPZBU, what does
HDWSNSF mean?

_____

 **Puzzle Pointer**

In this example, every
individual letter has a
different code system.

If the code for TROUSERS is GILFHVIH,
what does HDVZGVIH mean?

_____

Tricky

These four children have all created nets to make cubes. One child has made a mistake. Find out which net won't make a cube.

Now draw the missing images on other three children's cubes when the heart is on the top with its point towards you.

Fatimah's net

Rhea's net

Kai's net

Mal's net

The incorrect net is _____.

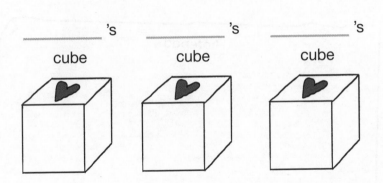

_____'s cube   _____'s cube   _____'s cube

Ava, Bear, Cali, Dev, Evie and Faz are all friends.
They each have a different age from 7 to 12.

Use the clues to work out how old each child is. You
can use the notepad as a working out area.

- Ava is older than Dev and younger than Faz.

- Cali is one year younger than Faz and one year
  older than Evie.

- Bear is neither the oldest nor the youngest, but
  he is older than Ava.

Tricky

Ava is   _____ .

Bear is   _____ .

Cali is   _____ .

Dev is   _____ .

Evie is   _____ .

Faz is   _____ .

Notepad

Add one letter each time to make a new word. You can move the letters around. There are clues to help.

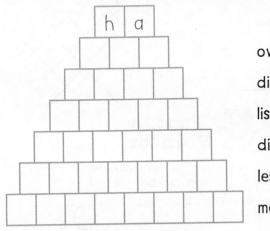

owned

difficult

listened

divided

less sunny

most robust

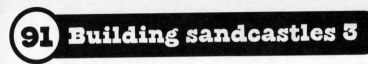

Puzzle Pointer

If you can't work out a word, move on to the next one, and then go back to it.

Tricky

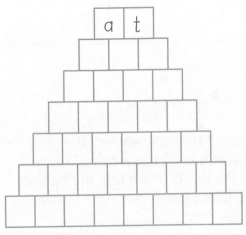

consume food

sporting group

boiling water

learn a skill

small rivers

stutters

92 Odd one out

Which is the odd one out?

a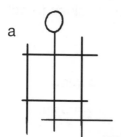

b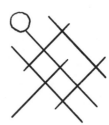

Puzzle Pointer

With images like this, always consider the shape, direction, number of lines/dots/internal shapes.

c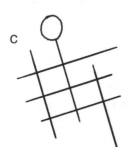

d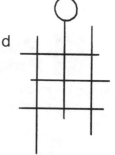

Example:

    a   b   c   d

c is the odd one out because each of the patterns has a ball on the top, each has a pair of parallel lines and when the ball is at the top, the base of the stem points to the left except for c where the stem points to the right.

Put these letters into the correct place on the windmill to find six hobbies that people do. The first letter of each word is given and they all share the same last letter. Use the picture clues to help you. They are harder this time!

a a a b c e g g i i i i i i i k k o m n n n n n n r s s t w w

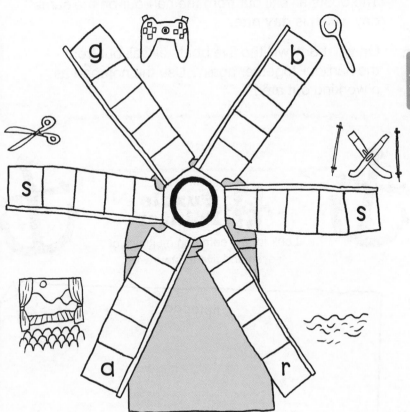

94 Sailing club

Five boats sail out from a harbour.

- The fishing trawler sails out every **seven** days.
- The transporter sails out every **five** days.
- The yacht sails out every **three** days.
- The cruise boat sails out every **two** days.
- The ferry sails out **every** day.

The boats all sail out from the harbour on the same day which is **day one**.

On what day will the five boats all sail out from the harbour together again? Use the notepad as a working out area.

Tricky

❓ Puzzle Pointer

Look for the common multiples of seven and five to start with.

Notepad

95 I do apologise...

Use the symbols and sounds to unlock the four famous 'sorry' sayings.

little, little, late, late

_____ _____ _____ _____

no X QQ it, it, it, it

_____ _____ _____ _____

x and lipstick, eyeshadow, blusher

_____ _____ _____ _____

give, give, give, give, and get, get, get, get

_____ _____ _____

Tricky

? Try this riddle: ?

I have no wings and I have no feet,
I have no aeroplane and I have no
string but I can climb high in the sky.

What am I?

Ten children have completed their end of year test. Use the clues to put the children in order from highest to lowest.

- Zach is one place ahead of Reuben and one place behind Brandon.

- Muhammad is not in the bottom two or the top two but he is ahead of Luna.

- Hurora is closer to the middle than Ivy.

- Chi is behind Luna but is before Ivy.

- Exactly four children did better than Brandon.

- Theo did better than Atticus, but Atticus was three places ahead of Reuben.

? Puzzle Pointer

Tick and cross the boxes as you read through the information to work out where everyone fits.

Tricky

	A	B	C	H	I	L	M	R	T	Z
1st										
2nd										
3rd										
4th										
5th										
6th										
7th										
8th										
9th										
10th										

1st _____

2nd _____

3rd _____

4th _____

5th _____

6th _____

7th _____

8th _____

9th _____

10th _____

Sudoku images 3

Look at these images:

Complete the grid by placing each of the nine images so that:

- each row has only one of each image
- each column has only one of each image
- each block of nine has only one of each image.

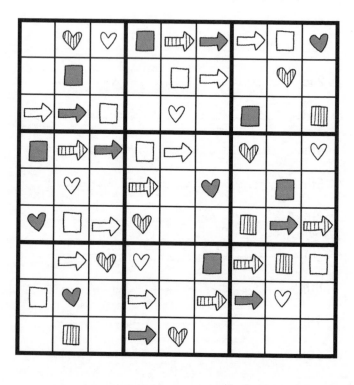

98 Tennis balls

Five tennis players are warming up by practising their racquet skills against a ball machine. Each player has set their ball machine to shoot balls at a different frequency.

- Bella's machine shoots a ball every minute.
- Joe's machine shoots a ball every 30 seconds.
- Tabitha's machine shoots a ball every $1\frac{1}{2}$ minutes.
- George's machine shoots a ball every 45 seconds.
- Owen's machine shoots a ball every 15 seconds.
- The five players begin at 10 a.m. and end at 10.16 a.m.

Tricky

How many times do they all hit a ball at the same time?

Notepad

117

99 Hide and seek 6x6

Hidden in the word search are six names of planets, seas and oceans, weather conditions, continents, rivers and mountains. Find the words and put them into their correct categories.

Planets	Seas and oceans	Weather conditions

Continents	Rivers	Mountains

Puzzle Pointer

Some of these words are quite tricky. You can research them online, look up the headings in books, check a dictionary or maybe ask other people.

Tricky

```
N E P T U N E T M H H B E I
M A S J E O N Z A A U L V W
A M I U A R I A T R R I E L
R A L P R T L M T A R Z R K
S Z E I T H E B E B I Z E I
S O U T H A M E R I C A S L
N N R E V M E Z H A A R T I
O X O R O E P I O N N D F M
W G P D L R C F R A E S U A
D A E A G I L R N T S A J N
O N N N A C O O S O D T I J
N G A U I A U S T R A L I A
Y E S B N O D T O N F A V R
I S I E D U Y Y R A R N E O
R P A C I F I C M D I T N R
I P U Z A Z L E Y O C I U P
S O B E N N E V I S A C S W
H S A T U R N E N O R T H R
```

Amal has folded up four sheets of paper and used a hole punch to make a pattern. Look at how Amal has folded the paper and then draw the pattern that she will see when she opens the paper up again.

1.

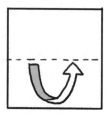

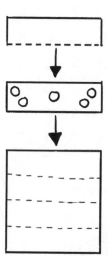

2.

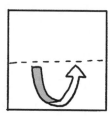

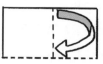

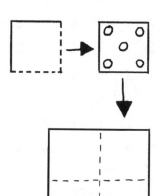

Tricky

Puzzle Pointer

The front of this paper is grey
and the back is white.

3.

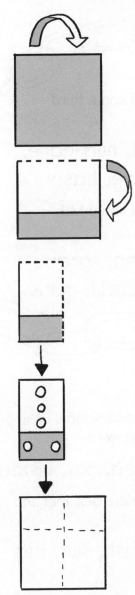

4.

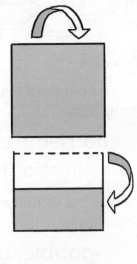

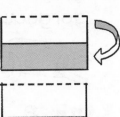

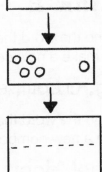

Tricky

101 The chain

Fix the broken links by solving the chain of puzzles.

Link 1

Underline the word that would come **third** alphabetically.

harried, hurried, hurricane,
horrid, horrible, hasty

Underline the word that would come **fifth** alphabetically.

gobble, grammar, grab,
gorgeous, graceful, gate

Link 2

Underline the word that fits before spoon, cake and time to make a new compound word.

big, cream, egg, tea, out, inside

Underline the word that fits before bell, mat and way to make a new compound word.

tool, door, out, fish, sun, big

Link 3

There are four buildings making up the four corners of a square. The baker's is east of the library and north of the school. The post office is west of the school and south of the library.

Which building is south east? The _____

Which building is north west? The _____

Link 4

There are four words but you only have the code for three of them. Can you match each code to the right word?

Words: PICNIC, PANICS, PAINTS, CATNIP

Codes: 123456, 624517, 625437

Which word do you not
have the code for? _____

What is the code for that word? _____

Now write the **last** letter from
each of the answer words here _____

Unscramble it it to complete the sentence below.

I can see the code word ⬚⬚⬚⬚⬚ .

102 Pick the lock 3

Here are five keys and five locks. Draw a line to match each key to the right lock.

Tricky

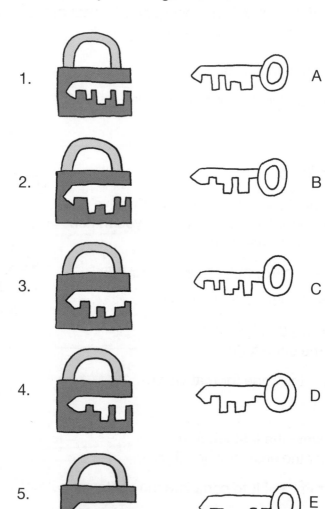

1.   A

2.   B

3.   C

4.   D

5.   E

Four children have drawn tiles, but some of each tile is missing. Draw the missing pieces in so that the patterns on the tiles are complete.

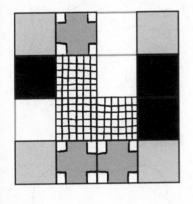

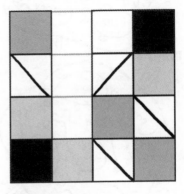

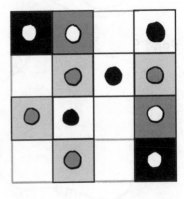

Tricky

Instead of six ponds with four fish in each, there are four ponds with six fish. Choose two fish from each pond that need to be moved into the empty ponds.

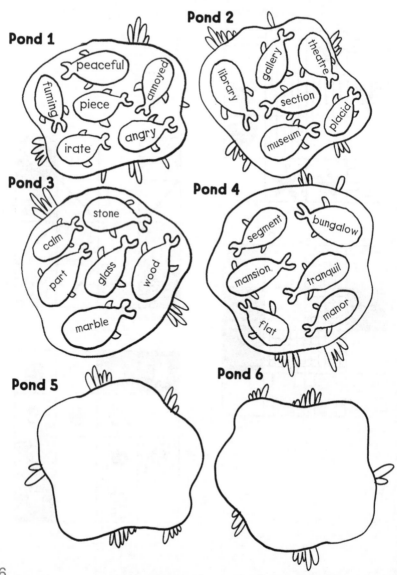

Pond 2

Pond 1

peaceful
annoyed
fuming
piece
irate
angry

library
gallery
theatre
section
placid
museum

Tricky

Pond 3

stone
calm
part
glass
wood
marble

Pond 4

segment
bungalow
mansion
tranquil
flat
manor

Pond 5

Pond 6

These baby aliens all look the same, but only two are **actually** the same. Find and circle the matching pair.

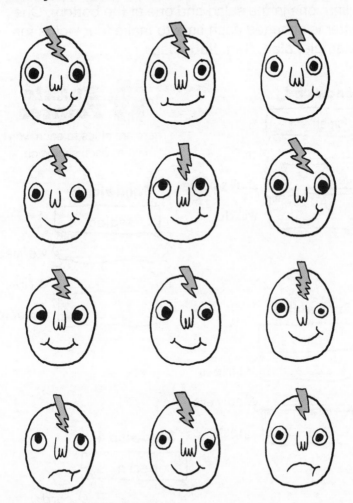

Tricky

Now see if you can make your own spot the baby alien puzzle for your friends. Make it really tricky by ensuring any differences are very subtle.

A café is selling four new word sandwiches. To make a sandwich there is a word on the top, one in the filling, one in the salad and one at the bottom. One letter is changed each time to make four words for example, **plan**, **flan**, **flap**, **clap**.

Sandwich 1

smelt

_____ sniff

_____ snail's home

_____ will do

Puzzle Pointer

There are clues to each word next to each sandwich.

Sandwich 2

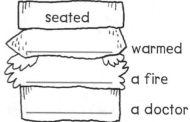

seated

_____ warmed

_____ a fire

_____ a doctor

Sandwich 3

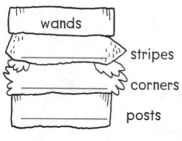

wands

_____ stripes

_____ corners

_____ posts

Sandwich 4

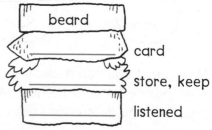

beard

_____ card

_____ store, keep

_____ listened

Tricky

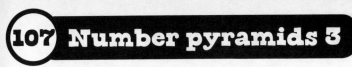

Sam and Sol are friends. Whatever Sam does Sol copies. Sam makes some number pyramids and Sol copies the same pattern.

In a number pyramid, the numbers on the lower levels determine the numbers above them. Fill in the missing numbers from Sol's pyramids.

Sam 1

Sol 1

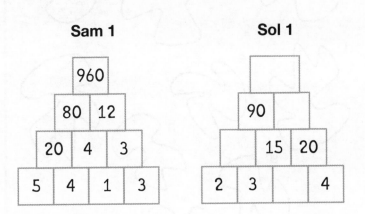

Sam 2

Sol 2

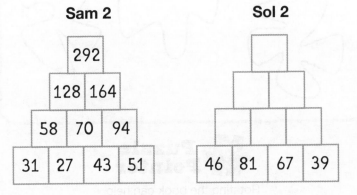

Tricky

There are four pairs of puzzle pieces plus three other puzzle pieces below. Find the three odd ones out.

Tricky

Puzzle Pointer

Rotating the book can help you see shapes from a different angle.

Tia is working out how much sugar is in her favourite foods. How many cubes are there?

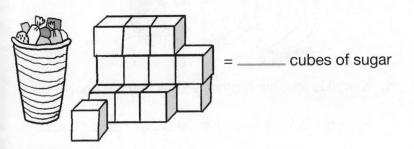 = _____ cubes of sugar

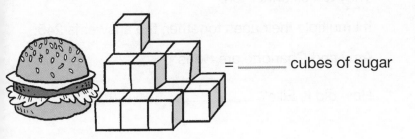 = _____ cubes of sugar

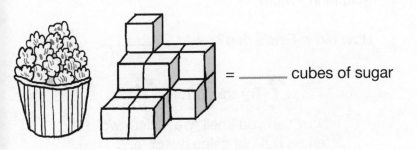 = _____ cubes of sugar

Tricky

1. Kamal is ten, his brother Vish is half his age.

   How old is Vish when Kamal is 20? _____

Tricky

2. There are three sisters: Ellie, Amy and Charlotte. They are all under ten.

   If I multiply their ages together, the answer is 245.

   Amy and Charlotte are twins.

   How old is Ellie? _____

3. Finn was ten last year. Next year, he will be a quarter of the age of his mum. Finn's dad is five years older than Finn's mum.

   How old is Finn's dad? _____

? Try this riddle: ?

How can you spell 'we' using two letters but not using 'w' or 'e'?

111 What comes next 2?

Draw what will come next in the box.

Tricky

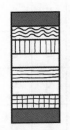    

? Puzzle Pointer

Be careful, they are not as easy as they seem.
Make sure you look at every part of each one
and see how it changes each time.

133

112 21s

Draw a circle around groups of numbers that total 21.

- You can't use a number more than once.
- Every number needs to be used.
- A group can be any size as long as every number inside adds up to 21.
- You can make a group horizontally, vertically or diagonally.

One has been done for you.

4	9	3	5	6	9	1	7	7	7
8	3	2	4	5	5	2	5	4	6
7	1	2	3	5	5	1	4	3	5
6	3	5	7	7	3	1	1	2	4
3	4	6	6	4	8	2	4	5	3
1	2	4	1	3	5	9	7	5	6
5	8	6	8	1	7	7	7	3	5
9	2	4	8	8	4	5	6	7	3

134

Tricky

Baljit has folded some paper and then cut out a shape. Draw what Baljit sees when he opens up the paper.

1.

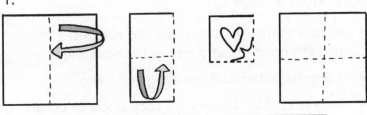

2.

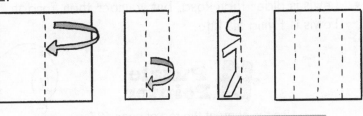

3.

Tricky

Five children aged from 7 to 11 are all different ages and each doing a different activity on the beach. Find how old each child is and the activity they are doing from these clues. Write the answers in the table at the bottom of page 137.

- Rosa is neither the oldest nor the youngest child and she is not flying a kite or rock-pooling.

- The youngest child is paddling in the sea.

- Ruby is 11. She is not at the rock pools or building sandcastles.

- Lewis is older than Rosa, but younger than Jordan. Lewis is flying his kite.

Tricky

 **Puzzle Pointer**

Use the chart at the top of page 137 to add ticks and crosses based on what you know.

CHILD	7	8	9	10	11	Ice cream	Kite flying	Paddling	Rock pools	Sandcastles
Rosa										
Lewis										
Harry										
Jordan										
Ruby										
Ice cream										
Kite flying										
Paddling										
Rock pools										
Sandcastles										

Tricky

	Age	Activity
Rosa		
Lewis		
Harry		
Jordan		
Ruby		

115 Clever copying

To enlarge a shape easily we can use grids. Just copy what is in each square and together the whole pattern will be larger.

Try copying the smaller patterns on the left to the grid on the right using the squares to help you.

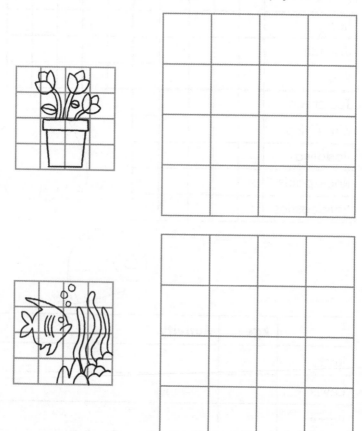

Why don't you make your own grid? Place it over any picture and then copy, enlarge or reduce the image.

116 Hidden image

There is an image hidden in this grid. To find it, the numbers tell you how many tiles are either shaded or are blank so 1 3 2 would be either:

  1 shaded, 3 blank and 2 shaded, or

  1 blank, 3 shaded and 2 blank.

The first column has been done for you.

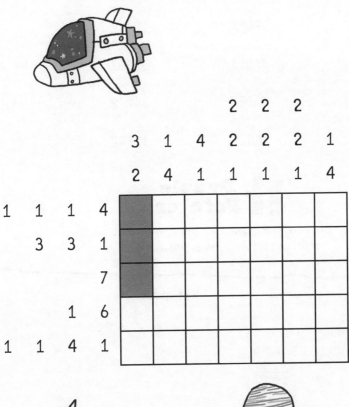

117 Coded names

Work out the code that represents each child's name.

Join the name to its correct code.

Names	Codes
AIDEN	52761
DANIA	24367
DIANA	12742
JANET	52367
JADEN	34272
TANIA	32742

Puzzle Pointer

Start by looking out for the names that
start or end with the same letters.

Tricky

Notepad

140

Puzzle power!

You've finished the tricky puzzles! Find out how well you did by checking the answers at the end of the book and add up how many tricky puzzles you got right. Score 2 for each fully correct puzzle, and 1 if you got some of the puzzle right. Then write down your total and read on to discover your puzzle power ...

My puzzle power score is ⟨ ⟩.

Puzzle power score 1–25

Well done! Go over some of the tricky puzzles and see if you can boost your score further.

Puzzle power score 26–49

Brilliant! You've zipped through the tricky puzzles. Pick out one or two of the puzzles you found challenging and give them another go.

Puzzle power score 50+

Wow! You have dazzling puzzle power! See if you can use your puzzle power to tackle *Bond Brain Training For Kids: Word Puzzles* and *Bond Brain Training For Kids: Number Puzzles*.

Answers

PAGES 6–7

1 Monster mash-up

Monster 1 should have a round face with round ears, eyes and nose, and the curved, smiling mouth.

Monster 2 should have a square face with square ears, eyes and nose, and a rectangular mouth.

Monster 3 should have a pentagon-shaped face with pentagon-shaped ears, eyes, nose and mouth.

 1 2 3

PAGES 8–9

2 What did I wear?

The 1st letter represents the top: a coat (A) a fleece (B) or a sleeveless top (C).

The 2nd letter represents the trousers: jeans (L), jogging trousers (M) or shorts (N).

The 3rd letter represents the hats: a peaked cap (X), a sunhat (Y) or a bobble hat (Z).

On Friday, the code **AMY** is a **coat, jogging trousers and a sunhat.**

PAGE 10

③ Fun at the zoo

Line **5** shows the visitor who did not follow the path.
The order is: **lion, elephant, seal, giraffe, monkey, bear, spider, parrot, snake**. Line 5 has the monkey after the snake and the lion after the spider.

PAGE 11

④ Pairs 1

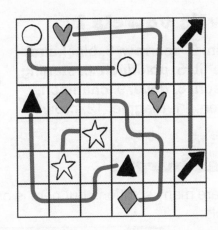

PAGE 12

⑤ Secret codes 1

The secret message reads:

Secret codes are fun as you can make any message encrypted.

PAGE 13

⑥ Mixed messages 1

The mixed message reads:

Can you read this message even when it looks so strange?

⑦ Cool running

Flick through your notebook and look at how your stick figure moves. Do you need to change some drawings to make it work properly? Show your finished animation to a friend!

⑧ Owl's vowels 1

1. **robin**, 2. **sparrow**, 3. **blackbird**,
4. **blue tit**, 5. **goldfinch**, 6. **starling**,
7. **pigeon**, 8. **dove**, 9. **chaffinch**,
10. **wren**, 11. **magpie**, 12. **crow**

⑨ Star burst 1

There are many solutions but here is one as an example:

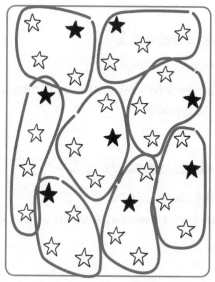

10 Mirror, mirror on the wall

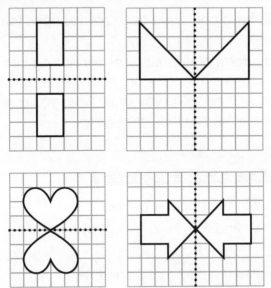

11 Shape-shifter 1

There are **16** triangles.

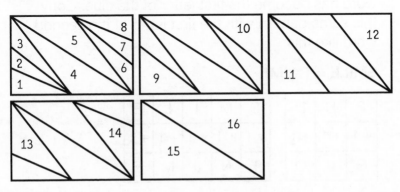

Box clever

Check you have only used geometric shapes to draw your picture.

Cubism is a form of art that turns everything into shapes – squares, triangles or circles, for example. Working in shapes helps you draw what you really see and not what you think you see.

 Riddle and rhyme 1

The answer to the riddle is **nerve**.

1st = N   2nd = E, N, Z, Y   3rd = R, E

4th = V, R   5th = E, S

The answer to the riddle is: an umbrella.

Follow the clues 1

To solve these clues, look at how the first letter of the word has become the first letter of the clue. Copy this same pattern with the first letter of the second word like this:

SMILE = TNJMF

F	U	N
+ 1	+ 1	+ 1
G	V	O

S	M	I	L	E
+ 1	+ 1	+ 1	+ 1	+ 1
T	N	J	M	F

HAPPY = GZOOX

S	A	D
–1	–1	–1
R	Z	C

H	A	P	P	Y
–1	–1	–1	–1	–1
G	Z	O	O	X

DPME = COLD

X	B	S	N
–1	–1	–1	–1
W	A	R	M

D	P	M	E
–1	–1	–1	–1
C	O	L	D

UZMR = VANS

B	Z	Q	R
+ 1	+ 1	+ 1	+ 1
C	A	R	S

U	Z	M	R
+ 1	+ 1	+ 1	+ 1
V	A	N	S

PAGE 20

15 Stable chaos

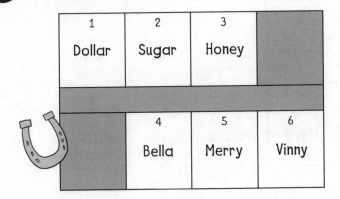

16 Sugar cubes 1

The cup of juice has **7** cubes of sugar.
The ice cream has **13** cubes of sugar.
The doughnut has **12** cubes of sugar.

17 Building sandcastles 1

be, bet, beat, beast, breast
it, sit, suit, suite, suited
as, has, hats, chats, cheats
to, toe, tore, store, stored

18 Windmill words 1

The words on the windmill are: **range**, **shape**, **angle**, **scale**, **metre**, **litre**.

19 Meerkat meeting

1	2	3	4
Brains	Lofty	Mini	Timid
5	6	7	8
Cyril	Vicious	Spike	Dave

㉚ Birthday cards

The answer is **CELEBRATE**.

From oldest to youngest: Cade, Elliot, Baahir, Rosie, Lydia.

㉑ Sudoku images 1

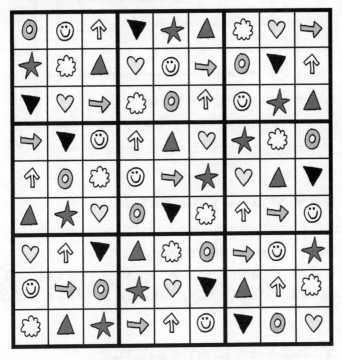

Colour names

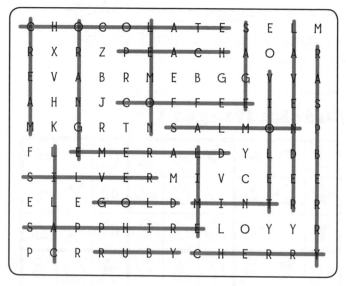

 Say what you see 1

Say the words out loud to hear the answers.

1. **Rob**, 2. **Joy**, 4. **Ray**, 5. **Katy**, 6. **Barry**

1. D + ear = **deer**, 2. C + 'at' = **cat**, 3. ELE + fan + T = **elephant**, 4. DON + key = **donkey**, 5. sea + L = **seal**.

 Find the trapeziums

Ceiling light shade, lamp shade, four flowers, plant pot, eight to make four hexagons to decorate the table, the table, the table stand.

Pick the lock 1

1.**C**, 2.**A**, 3.**D**, 4.**B**.

 It is rocket science!

The robots do something together **four** times. All of the timings are at multiples of 20 minutes.

9 a.m., 9.20 a.m., 9.40 a.m. and 10 a.m.

Corner conundrum 1

㉘ Fishy business 1

Pond 1: **fog, snow, rain, wind**

Pond 2: **jetty, quay, harbour, pier**

Pond 3: **nutmeg, pepper, paprika, ginger**

Pond 4: **carrot, potato, leek, onion**

Pond 5: **ash, beech, oak, rowan**

㉙ Word sandwiches 1

Sandwich 1: **fresh, flesh, flash, flask**

Sandwich 2: **mesh, mess, mass, mask**

Sandwich 3: **story, store, shore, chore**

Sandwich 4: **gloom, groom, broom, brood**

㉚ Book building 1

Shelf 1: The pattern is AB, CD, EF. **GH** and **IJ** continue the pattern. Each book in the pattern contains the next two letters in the alphabet. Here are two possible book titles: *Good Homes* and *Iced Jellies*.

Shelf 2: The pattern is ZA, YB, XC. **WD** and **VE** continue the pattern. The first letter of each book (Z, Y, X) is – 1 each time. The second letter of each book (A, B, C) is + 1 each time. Here are two possible book titles: *Wild Dogs* and *Volcano Eruptions*.

Shelf 3: The pattern is JB, LD, NF. **PH** and **RJ** continue the pattern. The first letter of each book (J, L, N) is + 2 each time. The second letter of each book (B, D, F) is + 2 each time. Here are two possible book titles: *Photographing Horses* and *Real Jam*.

Shelf 4: The pattern is MV, GB, AH. **UN** and **OT** continue the pattern. The first letter of each book (M, G, A) is – 6 each time. The second letter of each book (V, B, H) is + 6 each time. Here are two possible book titles: *Unique Nature* and *Old Times*.

PAGE 38

31 Number pyramids 1

Judy 1   **Judy 2**

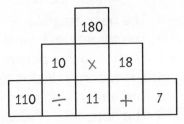

PAGE 39

32 Puzzle grid

Rhyme plus one 1

1. **starfish,** 2. **shoelace,** 3. **Yorkshire,** 4. **season,**
5. **onwards,** 6. **wallflower,** 7. **manmade,**
8. **hillside,** 9. **reddish.**

Spot the difference

In the second picture:

1. The heart is white
2. The trapezium is upside down
3. The star has a different number of points
4. The moon is upside down
5. The arrow is pointing in a different direction
6. The horizontal lines on the right-of-centre shape are now vertical
7. The top left-hand corner triangle has vertical stripes instead of horizontal
8. The top right-hand arrowhead does not have any dots
9. The hexagon has been replaced by an octagon.

 Dotty dominoes 1

1. There are **12** dominoes with an odd number of dots.

2. There are **6** dominoes with the same number of dots on both sides.

3. The answer is **6**.

4. If you have drawn dominoes with **6** dots, you are correct! (0,6), (1,5), (2,4), (3,3).

36 **Paper snowflakes 1**

1. 2. 3. 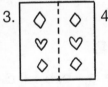 4.

37 **Production line 1**

38 **Transformers**

The ice cream has turned from plain ice cream to one with dots and one flake. Option **C** is the correct answer.

The arrow pointing to the right is now pointing to the left, the white colour has been changed to vertical stripes and the size has been made smaller. Option **D** is the correct answer.

The flat black oval has become the top of a white 3D cylinder so the flat black rectangle transforms into the top of a white cuboid with a rectangular top. Option **B** is the correct answer.

39 Gift wrapping

1.**C**, 2.**A**, 3.**D**, 4.**B**

40 Pairs 2

The pairs are: a + o, b + l, c + d, e + p, f + i, g + j, h + m, q + k. Shape **n** does not have a matching pair.

41 Food favourites

Child	Food	Place
Ava	Lasagne	Dad's house
Kishor	Curry	Mimi's house
Fin	Ice cream	Nice Ices
Kimmy	Burger	Mr Burger
Owen	Soup	Granny's house

PAGE 52

 Picture codes

Code 1: The first letter is the direction of the heart. **Upright is A** and **upside down is B**.

The second letter is the colour of the heart. **Checked is L, white is M** and **black is N**.

The third letter is the shape underneath. **W is a circle, X is a triangle** and **Y is a diamond**.

The missing code has an upright heart (A) is black (N) and has a triangle below (X) so the answer is **ANX**.

Code 2: The first letter of the bird is the beak. **S is long and thin, T is wide and large** and **U is small**.

The second letter is the length of the log below. **K is short, L is long** and **M is medium**.

The third letter is the direction of the eyeballs. **D is downwards, E is upwards** and **F is looking inwards**.

The missing code has a small beak (U), long log (L) and inward eyes (F) so the answer is **ULF**.

Code 3: The first letter refers to the outside shape. **N is oval, O is rectangular** and **P is hexagonal**.

The second letter is the colour of the outside shape. **U is vertical lines, V is horizontal lines** and **W is solid black**.

The third letter is the direction of the arrow. **T points upwards, S points downwards**.

The missing code has a rectangle background (O) with vertical lines (U) and a downwards pointing arrow (S) so the answer is **OUS**.

Secret codes 2

The secret message reads:

Writing in secret code is a great way of sending messages. Create your own secret codes to challenge your friends.

 Mixed messages 2

The letters are alternating between the two sentences so every other letter makes the proper sentence. If you look at the last line you can nearly see the word 'sentences' with each letter written twice. Add in the spaces so that the sentences can be easily read.

To resolve this we need to write out every other letter to make our two sentences. Then we need to work out where the spaces should go to make sense of the sentences.

 Pattern popping

The last two shapes on the fourth row – **the white triangle and the small dotted circle** – have swapped places.

 Owl's vowels 2

1. **potato**, 2. **carrot**, 3. **parsnip**, 4. **leek**,
5. **onion**, 6. **cabbage**, 7. **cauliflower**, 8. **broccoli**,
9. **spinach**, 10. **bean**, 11. **sweetcorn**, 12. **sprout**

Boxes

Each shape needs to have an area of 16 squares.
Here is one example:

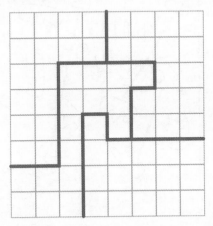

Park path

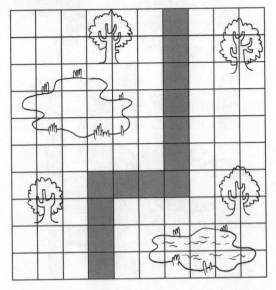

Puzzle pairs 1

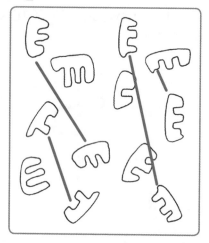

PAGES 60–1

 Shipping lanes

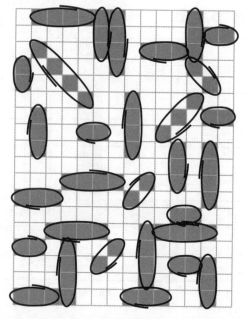

PAGE 62

51 Shape-shifter 2

There are other solutions but here is one as an example:

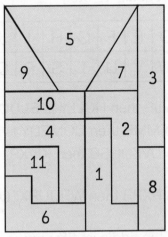

PAGE 63

52 Riddle and rhyme 2

My whole lasts for months, can you find the reason?
An example is 'winter', my word is **season**.

Follow the clues 2

These codes are mirror images. Here is the alphabet with the 1st half matching their alphabet pair in the 2nd half so 'A' equals 'Z' etc.

A	B	C	D	E	F	G	H	I	J	K	L	M
Z	Y	X	W	V	U	T	S	R	Q	P	O	N

If BERRY is YVIIB then HOLLY is **SLOOB**.

If FUNNY is UFMMB then COMEDY is **XLNVWB**.

If WEALTHY is DVZOGSB then KIVXRLFH is **PRECIOUS**.

If TRICKY is GIRXPB then WRUURXFOG is **DIFFICULT**.

The answer to the riddle is: **fifty coins**.

 Map matching

This is the correct building. The ridge of the triangular roof would show as a straight line and the two metal railings would show as one long, thin rectangle. The fifth picture is not correct as the large part of the building goes the wrong way.

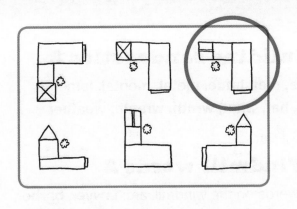

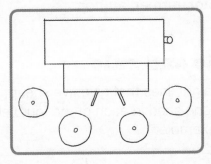

PAGE 66

55 The Kitten Hotel

1 Pumpkin	2 Tiger
	4 Bodkin
3 George	6 Snowball
5 Fluffy	
7 Jasper	8 Abby

56 Building sandcastles 2

1. me, met, tame, metal, mental, laments
2. at, hat, what, wrath, wreath, weather

57 Windmill words 2

The words on the windmill are: **lawyer, barber, waiter, doctor, farmer, author.**

58 Divide and rule

Any two straight lines that give five sheep, one water trough and one shed in each of the four fields. Here is an example:

Football fun

1st: Tranmere Rovers
2nd: Everton,
3rd: Chelsea
4th: Manchester City
5th: Liverpool
6th: Swansea City
7th: Wolverhampton Wanderers
8th: Nottingham Forest
9th: Sunderland
10th: Southampton

To solve this we can fill in the chart with all the potential teams.

Chelsea was beaten by two teams so Chelsea must come 3rd.

Nottingham Forest did better than two teams so they must come 8th.

Manchester City was one point higher than Liverpool so they can't be 10th and Liverpool can't be 1st.

Manchester City was two points lower than Everton, so Manchester City can't be 1st or 2nd. Everton can't be 10th or 9th.

Using similar processes, we can solve the puzzle.

60 Sudoku images 2

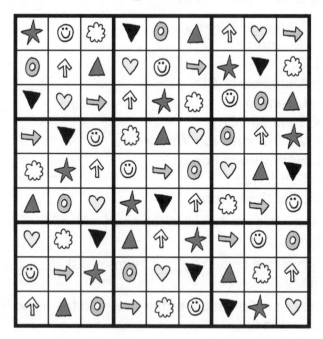

61 Hide and seek 5x5

Sport: **football, cricket, golf, rugby, tennis**
Language: **Arabic, French, Spanish, Chinese, Greek**
Food: **rice, pasta, bread, cheese, gravy**
Instrument: **guitar, piano, violin, trumpet, flute**
Book: **poetry**, **play, novel, factual, dictionary**

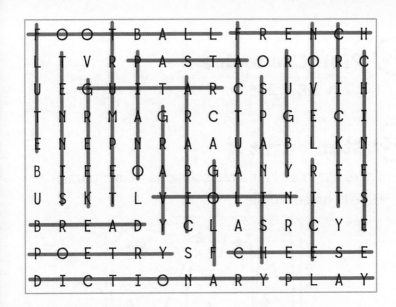

PAGE 73

62 3D printing

The 3D print outs match these drawings:
1. **C,** 2. **A,** 3. **B**.

PAGES 74–5

63 Paper punch 1

For each of these, the pattern of holes will be reflected in the vertical and horizontal line.

Pattern 1 will look like **B**.

Pattern 2 will look like **B**.

Pattern 3 will look like **A**.

Pattern 4 will look like **D**.

PAGE 76

64 Pick the lock 2

1.**C**, 2.**A**, 3.**B**, 4.**E**, 5.**D**

PAGE 77

65 Star burst 2

There are lots of different solutions to this puzzle.
Here is one example:

PAGE 78

66 Corner conundrum 2

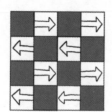

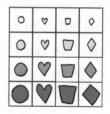

 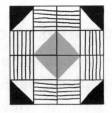

PAGE 79

67 **Missing half**

PAGE 80

68 **Fishy business 2**

Pond 1: **lavender, lilac, purple, violet**
Pond 2: **coffee, hot chocolate, soup, tea**
Pond 3: **mate, pal, ally, friend**
Pond 4: **diamond, sapphire, emerald, ruby**
Pond 5/6: **salsa, street dance, ballet, tap**
Pond 6/5: **agile, pliable, flexible, elastic**

 Word sandwiches 2

Sandwich 1: **chops, shops, ships, slips**

Sandwich 2: **plump, slump, stump, stamp**

Sandwich 3: **clown, crown, crows, brows**

Sandwich 4: **toaster, toasted, roasted, roosted**

Book building 2

Shelf 1: The pattern is AH, DK, GN. **JQ** and **MT** continue the pattern.

The first letter (A, D, G is + 3) each time. The first letter of the second word (H, K, N) is also + 3 each time. Here are two possible book titles: *Joinery Quiz* and *Making Tools*.

Shelf 2: The pattern is ZA, EV, JQ. **OL** and **TG** continue the pattern. The first letter (Z, E, J is + 5) each time. The first letter of the second word (A, V, Q) is – 5 each time. Here are two possible book titles: *Only Laughing* and *Two Ghosts*.

Shelf 3: The pattern is LI, JK, HM. **FO** and **DQ** continue the pattern. The first sequence is L, J, H, which is – 2 each time. The second sequence is I, K, M, which is + 2 each time. Here are two possible book titles: *Fruit Orchards* and *Dutch Queens*.

Shelf 4: The pattern is DF, HB, LX. **PT** and **TP** continue the pattern. The first sequence is D, H, L, which is + 4 each time. The second sequence is F, B, X, which is – 4 each time. Here are two possible book titles: *Possum Training* and *Taming Panthers*.

71 Number pyramids 2

Nykia 1

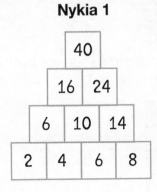

40	
16	24

6	10	14

2	4	6	8

Nykia 2

240	
12	20

6	2	10

6	1	2	5

72 Rhyme plus one 2

quicksand, blueberry, downstairs, boatyard or boathouse, farmhouse or farmyard, manage, upon, busking, sheepskin

73 What comes next 1?

Pattern 1: The number of sides on the shapes go up from three to four to five to six, and they alternate white and black. The missing shape should be white and have seven sides.

Pattern 2: The pattern is an increasing number of loops so the missing shape will have five loops. This is one example.

Pattern 3: The rectangles remain in sequence but moving up one position each time.

PAGE 87

74 Dotty dominoes 2

1. The number of dominoes with more than 8 dots is **6**.

2. The number of dominoes with fewer than 6 dots is **11**.

3. The answer is **5**.

4. If you have drawn dominoes with **5** dots, you are correct! (0,5), (1,4), (2,3).

PAGE 88

75 Paper snowflakes 2

1. 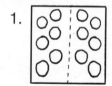 2.   3.

Production line 2

Pattern 1: The cupcake case has lines alternating vertical and horizontal. Every even-numbered cake has horizontal lines.

The top section alternates solid colour and dotted. Every even-numbered cake has dots.

The top leaf points left, then right, then no leaf. Every third cake has no leaf. As 18 is a multiple of 3, the 20th cake is second in this pattern.

The 20th cup cake has horizontal lines on the cupcake case, a dotted top section and a leaf pointing to the right, like this:

Pattern 2: The pictures alternate between a sandwich and a bagel. Every even-numbered tray has a bagel.

The fruit rotates apple, grapes and pear. As 18 is a multiple of 3, the 20th cake is second in this pattern.

The drinks rotate short drink and a tall drink. Every even-numbered tray has a tall drink.

The 20th picture has a bagel, grapes and tall drink, like this:

The cakes follow this pattern: top and base the same wavy pattern, base wavy and top white, top wavy and base white and top and base all white. As 20 is a multiple of 4, the 20th cake is fourth in this pattern.

The stars alternate between white and black. Every even-numbered cake has a black star.

The 20th cake has a black star and is all white, like this:

The bowls alternate between short and tall. Every even-numbered bowl will be tall.

The bowl shapes have the pattern curved, curved, trapezium, trapezium. As 20 is a multiple of 4, every fourth bowl will be a trapezium.

The food sequence is chips, chips, potatoes, potatoes. As 20 is a multiple of 4, the 20th cake is fourth in this pattern.

The colour of the bowls rotates white, grey, black.

As 18 is a multiple of 3, the 20th bowl is second in this pattern.

The 20th picture in the sequence has a tall trapezium bowl, in grey, with potatoes, like this:

77 Reading it any way

The sentences read:

We get so used to seeing words in just one direction.
But this shows you just how clever your brain is to still make sense of it.
If you can read it, you must have a genius brain!

78 Craft creation

Check you have followed the instructions correctly.

79 Dance partners

Dancer	Dance	Partner
Amy	Cha cha cha	Parva
Bella	Waltz	Angelo
Enya	Jive	Tom
Zuri	Salsa	Marco
Lian	Foxtrot	Harry

(80) Alien codes

Code 1: The first letter is the mouth: **A is smiling** and **B is a sausage shape**.

The second letter is the nose: **J is pointed**, **K is rounded** and **L is small**.

The third letter is the number of eyes: **P is 1**, **Q is 2** and **R is 3**.

The answer is **AJQ**.

Code 2: The first letter is the eyes: **S is different shapes**, **T is the same shape**.

The second letter is the smile: **J is a wide smile**, **K is a narrow smile**.

The third letter is the ears: **G is for triangular**, **H is for the antenna**, **F is for rounded**.

The answer is **SKF**.

Code 3: The first letter is the mouth: **Z has teeth**, **Y is a semicircle** and **X is a rectangle**.

The second letter is the nose: **D is U-shaped**, **E is a hook** and **F is straight lines**.

The third letter is the face shape: **L is a pentagon**, **M is a tear drop shape** and **N is oval**.

The answer is **ZEN**.

81 Secret codes 3

The secret message reads:
Can you use your powers of logic to solve this secret code?

82 Kitty competition

Three cats have both a tag and a bell: Snowdrop, Fifi and Colin.

One cat has neither a tag nor a bell: Joe.

The winner is **Snowdrop**.

	Colour	Tag	Bell
Boo Boo	Silver	Yes	No
Joe	Blue	No	No
Peaches	Red	No	Yes
Snowdrop	Yellow	Yes	Yes
Fifi	Pink	Yes	Yes
Colin	Green	Yes	Yes

 **18s**

There are lots of solutions to this puzzle. Here is one:

84 Mixed messages 3

Sometimes our brain will make sense of words with numbers in them to replace some letters.

Sometimes the sentences might be missing some of the letters and still our brain can make sense of them.

Even stranger is when our brain takes the really bizarre combination of letters, numbers and symbols and still, we can manage to make sense of it.

PAGE 102

85 Owl's vowels 3

1. **football**, 2. **baseball**, 3. **basketball**, 4. **rounders**,
5. **tennis**, 6. **cricket**, 7. **snooker**, 8. **hockey**,
9. **swimming**, 10. **badminton**, 11. **scuba diving**,
12. **rowing**, 13. **horse riding**, 14. **archery**

PAGE 103

86 Say what you see 2

1. **More often than not it is too difficult to see the bigger picture.**
2. **Reading between the lines is too tricky for people.**
3. **I think this is too funny for words!**

PAGE 104

87 Shape-shifter 3

There is more than one answer to this puzzle. Here is one example:

Follow the clues 3

RADIO = QZCHN

M	U	S	I	C
– 1	– 1	– 1	– 1	– 1
L	T	R	H	B

R	A	D	I	O
– 1	– 1	– 1	– 1	– 1
Q	Z	C	H	N

PURPLE = QVSQMF

O	R	A	N	G	E
+ 1	+ 1	+ 1	+ 1	+ 1	+ 1
P	S	B	O	H	F

P	U	R	P	L	E
+ 1	+ 1	+ 1	+ 1	+ 1	+ 1
Q	V	S	Q	M	F

HDWSNSF = FESTIVE

D	Z	R	P	Z	B	U
– 2	+ 1	– 4	+ 1	– 5	+ 3	– 1
B	A	N	Q	U	E	T

H	D	W	S	N	S	F
– 2	+ 1	– 4	+ 1	– 5	+ 3	– 1
F	E	S	T	I	V	E

If TROUSERS is GILFHVIH, then HDVZGVIH is
SWEATERS. (This is a mirror image so A = Z etc.)

 Clever cubes

Mal's net cannot make a cube.

Fatimah's
Cube

Rhea's
Cube

Kai's
Cube

PAGE 108

90 How old are we?

Ava is 8, Bear is 9, Cali is 11, Dev is 7, Evie is 10 and Faz is 12.

PAGE 109

91 Building sandcastles 3

1. **ha, had, hard, heard, shared, shadier, hardiest**

2. **at, eat, team, steam, master, streams, stammers**

PAGE 110

92 Odd one out

Pattern **d** is the odd one out. It has four internal rectangles but the others have three.

PAGE 111

93 Windmill words 3

The words on the windmill are: **gaming, baking, skiing, rowing, acting, sewing.**

Sailing club

The five boats will all sail out from the harbour together again on day 211.

The boats all leave on day 1 so our multiples will always be plus 1.

The fishing trawler and transporter are the first boats to consider so we are looking for multiples of 7 that are also multiples of 5. This means we are looking for multiples of 35.

The next boat to match to multiples of 35 is the yacht which is every 3 days so the first multiple of 35 that is also a multiple of 3 is 210.

The cruise boat is every other day beginning on day 1 so we are looking for an odd number. The ferry sails out every day.

As all the boats sailed together on day 1, add 1 day to 210 to find the answer **211**.

 I do apologise...

Too little too late, No excuse for it, Kiss and make up, Forgive and forget.

The answer to the riddle is: **I am smoke**.

 Testing times

1st = Theo, 2nd = Hurora, 3rd = Muhammad, 4th = Atticus, 5th = Brandon, 6th = Zach, 7th = Reuben, 8th = Lauren, 9th = Chi, 10th = Ivy

PAGE 116

97 Sudoku images 3

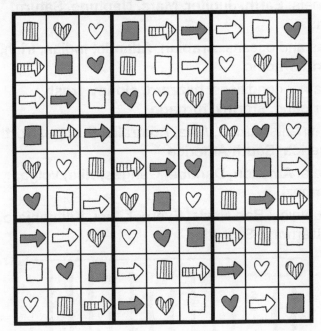

PAGE 117

98 Tennis balls

If they start their machines at 10 a.m. and end at
10.16 a.m. **they will all hit a ball at the same time
6 times**, at 10.00 a.m and then every three minutes.

99 Hide and seek 6x6

Planets: **Earth, Jupiter, Mars, Neptune, Saturn, Venus**

Seas and oceans: **Arabian, Atlantic, Indian, Irish, North, Pacific**

Weather conditions: **blizzard, cloudy, frosty, hurricane, stormy, tornado**

Continents: **Africa, Asia, Australia, Europe, North America, South America**

Rivers: **Amazon, Danube, Ganges, Nile, Volga, Zambezi**

Mountains: **Ben Nevis, Everest, Fuji, Kilimanjaro, Matterhorn, Snowdon**

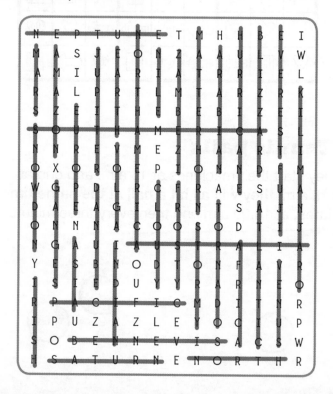

100 Paper punch 2

When Amal unfolds the paper, these are the patterns she will see:

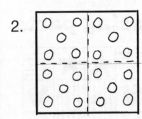

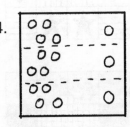

101 The chain

Link 1: **horrible, graceful**

Link 2: **tea, door**

Link 3: **school, library**

Link 4: **PANICS = 624517, PAINTS = 625437, CATNIP = 123456.**

The word you do not have the code for is **PICNIC**.
The code is **651451**.

I can see the code word **clearly**.

185

PAGE 124

102 Pick the lock 3

1.**C**, 2.**E**, 3.**D**, 4.**B**, 5.**A**

PAGE 125

103 Missing parts

 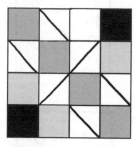

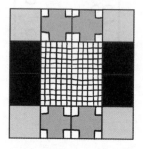 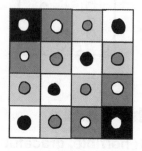

PAGE 126

104 Fishy business 3

Pond 1: **irate, annoyed, angry, fuming**
Pond 2: **museum, gallery, theatre, library**
Pond 3: **glass, stone, marble, wood**
Pond 4: **mansion, bungalow, manor, flat**
Pond 5/6: **peaceful, placid, calm, tranquil**
Pond 6/5: **piece, section, part, segment**

105 Spot the baby alien

The matching pair includes the first alien on the first row and the third alien on the second row.

106 Word sandwiches 3

Sandwich 1: **smelt, smell, shell, shall**

Sandwich 2: **seated, heated, heater, healer**

Sandwich 3: **wands, bands, bends, sends**

Sandwich 4: **beard, board, hoard, heard**

107 Number pyramids 3

Sol 1

		27000			
	90		300		
6		15		20	
2	3		5		4

Sol 2

		529			
	275		254		
127		148		106	
46	81		67		39

108 Puzzle pairs 2

The matching pairs are: a + k, b + j, c + h, d + f.
The odd pieces out are **e**, **g** and **i**.

109 Sugar cubes 2

The cup of sweets has **15** cubes of sugar.

The hamburger has **17** cubes of sugar.

The bowl of popcorn has **16** cubes of sugar.

110 Logical thinking

1. **Vish will be 15.** (He is five years younger than Kamal.)

2. Amy and Charlotte are seven so **Ellie is five**.

We have to find the prime factors of 245 which are 5 x 7 x 7.

3. **Finn's dad is 52** (Finn is 11 now, next year he will be 12 and his mum will be 48 which means she is now 47. His dad is five years older so he is 52.)

The answer to the riddle is: **We can write 'us'**.

111 What comes next 2?

The shapes are adding **one extra black dot each time, removing one white triangle each time and the stars alternate black and white.**

The final box should have **6 black dots, 1 white triangle and a black star**. This is one possibility:

The string has one more bend on the right-hand side each time but one fewer bead each time.

The final box should have a string with 5 bends to the right and no bead like this:

The bottom grey bar alternates each time. The other bands move down one place lower each time.

The final box should have these patterns running top to bottom: horizontal stripe, white, checked, white, grey, waves, vertical stripe, grey like this:

21s

There is more than one answer to this puzzle.
Here is an example:

4	9	3	5	6	9	1	7	7	7
8	3	2	4	5	5	2	5	4	6
7	1	2	3	5	5	1	4	3	5
6	3	5	7	7	3	1	1	2	4
3	4	6	6	4	8	2	4	5	3
1	2	4	1	3	5	9	7	5	6
5	8	6	8	1	7	7	7	3	5
9	2	4	8	8	4	5	6	7	3

113 Paper snowflakes 3

1.   2.    3.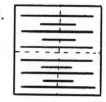

PAGES 136–7

14 Day at the beach

	Age	Activity
Rosa	8	Sandcastles
Lewis	9	Kite flying
Harry	7	Paddling
Jordan	10	Rock pools
Ruby	11	Ice cream

PAGE 138

15 Clever copying

Check you have drawn in the correct squares to enlarge the images.

PAGE 139

16 Hidden image

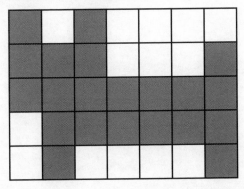

117 Coded names

Aiden = 24367
Dania = 32742
Diana = 34272
Janet = 52761
Jaden = 52367
Tania = 12742

A = 2, D = 3, E = 6, I = 4, J = 5, N = 7, T = 1

Notepad
